MW00943294

ALWAYS A NEXT ONE

PRAISE FOR JOHN L. LEONARD'S

ALWAYS A NEXT ONE
TRUE STORIES OF DOG FOSTERING

2013 Readers' Favorite
International Book Awards
Gold Medal Winner

"Always a Next One is a wonderfully written story of a family's involvement with taking in foster animals until their permanent homes are found. Readers who like Herriot's animal stories will be drawn to John Leonard's writings and will want to read more than the sample chapter of dog stories featuring Leonard's beloved Ox at the book's end. The writing in each story is consistent and not maudlin and the animals' characters come through believably. Simone the cat is a cat, not a human in disguise. This is a book that belongs on animal lovers' reading lists everywhere."
–Alice D. for Readers Favorite, 5 stars

"I have always been a 'dog person' and knew I would enjoy the book, but it still surprised me how much I enjoyed it. The author wrote in a conversational manner, as if he were sitting with me and personally telling me his tales. I recommend this book with a sense of urgency.."
–Lee Ashford for Readers Favorite, 5 stars

ALWAYS A NEXT ONE

true stories of dog fostering

by

John L. Leonard

The actual events herein described are based on true stories involving real animals, and the community of volunteers dedicated to their rescue, rehabilitation, and adoption into permanent "forever" homes. In certain cases incidents, characters, and timelines may have been changed for dramatic purposes. Certain characters may be composites.

Copyright © 2012 John L. Leonard
www.southernprose.com

Published by Each Voice Publishing
www.eachvoicepub.com

All rights reserved. No part of this book may be reproduced or transmitted in any form or by any means, electronic or mechanical, including photocopying, recording, or by any information storage and retrieval system, without written permission from the author, except for the inclusion of brief quotations in a review.

All rights reserved.
ISBN: 978-1478205265

Cover Design: Lisa H. Leonard

INTRODUCTION

The stories you are about to read are true. Most of the names have not been changed because neither dogs nor cats can read. They can't sue me, either.

Our adventures began innocently enough. My wife Lisa decided to get involved in something besides work, family, and gardening. She thought working with homeless animals sounded rewarding. She always respected the work my own mother and aunt dedicated to the Humane Society in their hometown of Savannah, Georgia.

Lisa searched the internet, looking for a good place within driving distance to volunteer — a rescue group with a brick-and-mortar animal shelter location where she could interact with the animals directly. A no-kill Humane Society one county to our east caught her eye. She attended the next volunteer orientation listed on their event calendar. The orientation confirmed her hunch that this was the right place for her to help. She decided to jump in with both feet.

This would be the appropriate time for me to acknowledge that my wife is obsessive-compulsive, a perfectionist, and a perennial over-achiever. She never gets "somewhat" involved in anything. With her, it is all or nothing. As her father told me soon after we met, "Her spring is wound a little too tight."

She started by helping in the adoption center office on Thursday afternoons, getting agreement from her employer to take that community give-back time away from work each week. A few months passed and she worked her first Saturday offsite dog adoption event at the local Petsmart. I recognized that telltale gleam in her eye. This might soon overtake the fervor she felt for collecting native perennials for her garden. I was tired of digging holes in the hard red Georgia clay for her latest Piedmont Azalea specimens, so I innocently encouraged her.

Within another month, she received the first of what would be many frantic phone calls asking if we would foster a dog. We talked about the idea of bringing an unknown dog into our home, debated the risks, and weighed the commitment we expected it would require. We both feared we would become so attached we couldn't part with our first foster dog. We agreed to be firm in our resolve.

Looking back now, I can recognize the most popular recurring theme in these pleas for foster homes seemed to be that someone rescued a dog but *"can't keep it."*

The phrase *"can't keep it"* is actually a coded message for self-absolution that roughly translates, *"I can't be inconvenienced by caring for this animal while the shelter looks for other options. I did my good deed already by saving the dog/cat. I am not in this for the long term commitment of caregiving, just for the short term act of rescuing."*

I guess that sounds cynical. Time has taught me that animals have a lot more depth of character than most people do. I am reminded of Ranger, a beautiful German Shepherd Dog who found his forever home within a week or so of coming to our "safe house." His temporary name was inspired by the story behind his rescue; he had been tied to the bumper of a Ford Ranger truck by a rope since he was a young pup, with only a few feet to roam. The woman who convinced the owner to surrender the dog put him in her garage, mildly afraid of the large animal. Of course, she *"couldn't keep him."* She warned me as she opened the door to the garage, "He will jump on you."

I had just enough time to kneel down before the powerfully built young dog ran over me like a truck, exuberant that someone came to show him attention. An absolutely gorgeous dog that resembled our beloved Sheba, he found his perfect forever home within a week of coming into our foster care. His name eventually changed from Ranger to Rocco; his adoptive parents turned out to be fans of the Philadelphia Flyers and could not tolerate having their new dog evoke thoughts of their hockey rivals, the New York Rangers.

But I digress, jumping ahead in the sequence of our tales. Return with me to that first spin of our revolving door.

Prodded into action by that first desperate phone call and with the naive idealism of a new volunteer, Lisa cracked like a South Georgia pecan. We agreed to take in our first foster dog, billed as a "black lab puppy." Lisa met the woman who found but *"couldn't keep her"* in a grocery store parking lot later that day. She knew immediately the young dog looking up at her with hopeful eyes was in reality neither a Labrador nor a puppy. She was an undersized pit bull mix — known to be harder to place because of her breed.

We named her Lucy, took many adorable photographs, wrote up an appealing bio, and got it posted on the adoption website. Meanwhile, Lisa immersed herself in reading all she could find about the bully breeds and how to find them the best homes possible. I resigned myself to the idea we would have a long-term houseguest for an open-ended stay.

To our mutual surprise, a young couple adopted Lucy within a few short weeks, offering her a wonderful home with a male boxer companion. Her new family sent adorable pictures of Lucy snuggling with her new buddy. Just that fast... like a couple of dog-fostering junkies, we were hooked.

After a few more quick placements of dogs in similar need, Lisa announced that she wanted to select our next foster from the one of the dogs at risk of becoming stir crazy from their extended stay at the adoption center. Her heart went out to the dog that had been at the shelter the very longest, waiting in vain for someone to adopt him — until he grew apathetic about human interaction. The first of these "long-termers" to come home with Lisa was Trigger, a Treeing Walker Coonhound who spent several years as a yard dog at his previous home, stuck outside with very little human and no canine companionship.

Watching this institutionalized, emotionally detached dog transform into a loving, happy part of our family was one of the most rewarding experiences we'd had thus far. We rehabilitated Trigger and a young man looking for the perfect companion for his beagle soon adopted him. He also sent us a very nice note to say how happy the three of them were in Trigger's new forever home.

We were *really* hooked now.

And so for the next five years, our home transformed into a way station, a halfway house for dogs and cats in need. Sometimes an animal stayed with us overnight, others shared our home for months. On rare occasions, they became permanent members of our family.

Through the years, we replaced room after room of carpet with wood or tile floors. We gave up on the concept of having throw pillows on the furniture. Wearing black clothes without pet hair was inconceivable. Well-trodden pathways cut through previously manicured lawn in our back yard. Metal dog crates became end tables. The corner of every piece of wooden furniture proudly bore the teething marks of one puppy or another. Visits from old friends somehow didn't seem to last as long as they used to. We routinely threw an extra steak on the grill or chicken breast in the baking dish because, of course, our animal guests enjoyed a few special tidbits cut up and sprinkled over their kibble. The down side of such regal treatment is that some of our "temporary" guests recognized a good deal when they saw it and simply refused to leave. They remain with us.

On the flip side, we got much joy from watching a timid, frightened animal turn into a loving companion with just a bit of acceptance and consistency. We nursed back to health animals with everything from heartworms to broken bones and broken spirits. We stayed up all night feeding ice chips to puppies sick with Parvovirus, anxiously waiting for the vet's office to open. We felt the satisfaction of seeing one of our long-term fosters adopted into the one home that was the perfect fit for his quirky personality. We got happy email and phone updates from families who adopted our fosters, thanking us for helping them find their happy endings, with notes like "Reilly enjoys watching princess movies with our youngest daughter."

I learned more about dog training than I ever imagined possible. Integrating a new dog into our growing pack, housetraining puppies, teaching an unruly dog to walk nicely on leash… those roles fell more and more to me with time.

Our own dogs learned how to help the broken ones, too. They provided the example of stability and pack order that new dogs would learn to follow. They seemed to understand these visitors were to be accepted and helped.

Working with the animals that find themselves in the shelters and rescue programs is challenging. These are creatures whose lives are upended, their familiar surroundings taken away, their past lives often unpleasant or unknown. Healing hearts and minds takes as much or more patience than healing sick or injured bodies. The different approaches to doing so are as varied as the animals themselves. A lot of our rehabilitation techniques we learned through trial and error and sometimes I am sure we made a few well-intentioned mistakes. But no animal in our care ever suffered from a lack of love and attention.

Fostering isn't glamorous. We got used to driving around with extra blankets and towels in the car, learning the hard way that a stray dog is almost always dirty, smelly, and very likely to get carsick. He may hike his leg on the back door as you hold it open, encouraging him to go outside to do his business. His long nails will need trimming and his sore, untended ears will need a gentle cleaning. He will squirm and bolt away when you try to bathe him, quite sure you mean him harm with this strange new sensation of warm water and shampoo.

But fostering is exhilarating. Watching blank, sad eyes become lively and trusting makes it all worthwhile. Seeing a thin, bony ribcage fatten out with regular meals is satisfying. Watching a dog confined for months take his first full-speed, joyous sprint across the backyard will bring a smile on even the toughest of days.

New volunteers at the shelter often asked us, "How do you do it? I would get too attached. I don't think I could let them go."

Our ready response was always heartfelt, "I tell myself that if I keep this one, I can't help the next one. And there is a long line of animals out there needing our help. I don't keep this one because I know there is always a next one who needs me."

Over time, though, we did gradually add to our count of permanent pets. These were always the ones who were such outcasts that they were not adoptable into normal homes. The only place they seemed to fit in was in our home, on our "island of misfits."

In our journey through years of animal rescue, we've had the joy and honor of getting to know hundreds of dogs, cats, puppies, and kittens along the way. Some stay with us only briefly, but when I look into each hopeful set of eyes for the first time, I know the impact this creature will have on my life will be a lasting one. These stories are a few of our most memorable encounters.

Though I often blame or credit my wife, depending on the circumstance, the animals living in our house do so primarily because of *me*. I'm the one who melts at the sight of a furry face with pitiful eyes.

And they all look pitiful at dinnertime.

CHAPTER 1
THE CATFIGHT

My exposure to animal rescue began in my childhood. Looking back, I realize it seemed quite normal to me to get involved with our local Humane Society when my time came. My mother and aunt were heavily involved with the local shelter during my childhood, and as a result, all of our lives grew richer. Aunt Joyce claimed that she tried fostering animals, but she ended up keeping most of them. The household pets with which I grew up were almost all rescues from the Humane Society.

Many years of hard work by Mom and Aunt Joyce gave me a lifelong perspective on the value of life and the uniqueness of each living creature. Aunt Joyce blazed a trail for the family's involvement in volunteer work with animal rescue, but soon she got Mom involved by asking her to empty the donation banks on display in businesses near where my mother worked. That led to her helping with yard sales, and then to progressively increased involvement until Mom served four consecutive terms on the board of directors, alternating as president and vice president. My mother has now volunteered in one capacity or another for the Humane Society of Chatham County, Georgia, for over thirty years.

Fully immersed in volunteer work for the Humane Society during most of her adult life, when Aunt Joyce passed away, she left a legacy for the homeless animals of Savannah in the form of a new shelter building, constructed with donations made in her honor. For her funeral, in lieu of flowers, the family requested donations be made in her honor to our Humane Society. Aunt Joyce would have insisted on nothing else.

Later, when my dad died, we followed the precedent set with Aunt Joyce. Flowers would have been for us, not the dearly departed. Dad always said that he liked animals better than people.

Tasha was one of the very first animals of in ever-growing number of companions our family would adopt over the years. She taught me that friendship could flourish in the most unlikely of circumstances, as long as we keep an open mind about our differences.

The story you are about to hear is true. The names haven't been changed, because no one involved was innocent.

My name is Sparky. I go to Windsor Forest Elementary School, a block from home. I'm small for my age, a bookworm, and the teacher-appointed hall monitor. Mrs. Ward makes me wear a special sash with a badge. I have to wear it every day before school starts. She tells me I have to patrol the school grounds as students make their way to their homerooms. I am supposed to report kids who cause trouble, or pick on the smaller kids.

You could spell trouble C-O-L-E. My new job means that Cole Parker, twice my size and in the sixth grade, hates my guts.

"Hey, look at the little po-leeez-man. What's the matter, Sparky? Mrs. Ward couldn't make anybody else rat out their friends?" Cole laughed as he played to his audience of fellow troublemakers. Empowered by their snickers, Cole snatched my sash off over my head and twirled it above me, just out of my reach.

My friend Joey was another school patrol, my same age, but bigger than I was and not afraid of anything, or anybody. He seemed to appear out of nowhere, stepping between Cole and me.

"Give it back, or I'm gonna pound on you, Parker."

Nobody messed with Joey. Even Cole wasn't that stupid. He tried to act like he was only playing around, pretending he wasn't afraid of Joey and that it was no big deal to give back my sash, but everybody knew he was scared, just like me. I breathed a sigh of relief as I stooped to retrieve my sash. Joey walked down the hallway. The standoff was over.

Cole waited until Joey was out of earshot to lean in and growl, "You can't hide behind Joey's apron strings forever. Watch your back. One of these days, I'll catch you when he isn't around, and you are going to get a beating like you've never had before." Cole only picks fights that he is sure to win. He would enjoy beating up an easy target, a smaller kid like me.

I didn't bother pointing out to Cole that if he'd paid attention in English class, he would know that he just mixed his metaphor. I knew that Cole would not like me any better after I corrected his butchering of a cliché.

The very next day, I took Sheba for her usual walk. A beautiful and loyal German Shepherd Dog, Sheba outweighed me and was my best friend. To my surprise, Cole rode up on his bike and started taunting me again. He didn't throw any punches, but I guessed that was only because he was afraid of Sheba. He eyed her cautiously. At first Sheba looked at Cole with disinterest, but then she sensed my fear. Cole was not so afraid that he stopped taunting me. His evil intent soon became clear to Sheba. Her ears perked up, her senses on full alert.

"You got a beating comin', you little jerk. When I catch you without Joey or that stupid dog around, I'm going to pound you into the ground," he leered.

I mustered up enough false bravado to respond, "If you don't leave me alone, Sheba will bite you!"

Cole pretended he wasn't scared, but as he eyed my dog, he looked like just realized that he brought a knife to a gunfight. His words sounded more confident than his voice. "You can't make your dog bite me."

Because I was really afraid of Cole, I had to follow through with my threat. My heart beat hard in my chest and my fists clenched in determination. I realized I had no idea what would happen next, but I managed to cough out the words, "Sheba, sic 'em!"

With a serious, low growl, she lunged at Cole's bike, easily knocking him flat on the sidewalk. Sheba's quick reaction to my meek, almost desperate command scared me as completely as it scared the swagger out of Cole. He scrambled backward on his hands and feet, real fear blanching his face as he switched from predator to prey in an instant. When I grabbed Sheba's leash and pulled her back, she obeyed without hesitation. She understood the prostrate boy received her message, loud and clear. I was the one who fed and walked her every day. Don't mess with the food source. Cole clawed his way back to his feet and ran away, leaving his overturned bicycle unceremoniously sprawled across the sidewalk and curb.

The bully never bothered me again, not before, during, or after school.

And I now knew exactly how strong and powerful Sheba could be. I was very glad she did not bite Cole, because that would have meant trouble for both Sheba and me. I'd seen what she could do to a basketball. She could have really hurt Cole if she had bit him after my impulsive command. That thought scared me enough that I promised myself to never again test Sheba's restraint.

I had a basketball court in my back yard, but we didn't play there very often any more. Eight different times Sheba stole the basketball after someone missed a shot. When Sheba got the ball, no one got it back. She trapped it between her front paws, clamped down with her jaws, and carried it like a trophy until we tired of chasing her. Then Sheba chomped down on her prize — my basketball — until it rewarded her with a satisfying, "Pop." Eight of my basketballs met this same fate before I finally learned my lesson. Sheba didn't allow basketball if we weren't going to let her play. I couldn't afford to shoot hoops on my home court anymore.

As the school year faded into the hot, lazy days of summer break, so did the memory of my ill-advised use of Sheba to rid myself of my tormentor. Both dog and boy were equally surprised the day Mom brought home a Siamese cat from the shelter. Dad and I wondered if she had gone crazy. Sheba showed a disturbing fascination with our newest addition, and the new cat recognized Sheba's intent was not friendly. She apparently considered the cat an intruder into her domain, not our most recent addition to the family.

In an odd juxtaposition of royalty and comedy, the cat was hopelessly cross-eyed. Mom named her Tasha and spoiled her rotten. I tried to win her favor by offering her a small piece of my steak. She sniffed it, and then turned her back to me, haughtily raising her tail as if I had just insulted her. Mom watched and enlightened me, "She's not going to eat that. Tasha likes her steak rare." Like I said, Tasha the cross-eyed cat was being spoiled rotten.

Mom and Dad came up with a plan intended to keep Sheba and Tasha separated, to make sure Tasha wouldn't get hurt. Our dining room was in the middle of the house, next to the kitchen, and had doors on both ends. We closed the doors and checked to make sure the room was clear before letting the dog or the cat inside. For weeks this shell game of carefully orchestrated opening and closing doors allowed both Sheba and Tasha to live with our family, yet never directly face each other.

When the two animals finally came face-to-face, it was my fault. I checked the dining room for Tasha and was sure I didn't see her. Convinced I had followed the rules, I let Sheba in with me. We played with a tennis ball in Sheba's favorite game of keep-away. When I bounced the ball on the floor between us, I talked to her about there I might throw it next. Sheba's tail beat against a dining room chair like a drummer keeping time. Unnoticed by either of us, Tasha slept soundly in the chair. Sheba's thrashing tail beat her soundly in the head. The cat woke up, stretched out in slow motion, her paws behind her head. Like a flash of lightning, Tasha extended her claws, grabbed Sheba's tail, pulled it into her mouth, and bit down with a vicious growl. The shocked shepherd whirled around, her eyes wide with anger. She couldn't believe the cat had the nerve to bite her. I sucked in my breath, sure that Sheba was going to kill the cat.

But Sheba didn't retaliate. She just glared at Tasha, long and hard. I still held my breath. Tasha met her gaze calmly, acting as if she had done nothing wrong. Neither of them blinked, and I didn't dare, either. Sheba looked away first, feigning disinterest as she turned to search for the forgotten tennis ball. The cat apparently gained her respect.

However, we all still considered Tasha a bit hapless. Sure, she was fearless and considered herself a great squirrel hunter, but she really wasn't. Dad fed cracked pecans daily to the squirrels in the pine tree in our front yard. Tasha crouched in wait at the base of the tree. A squirrel ran down within a few feet of her, yet managed to evade the cat and get the pecans. Dad said Tasha's crossed eyes made her see two squirrels. She didn't know which one to chase. For me it was a source of improvised comedy. Sheba often joined me as I watched Tasha's tireless but futile efforts with great amusement. We both knew Tasha would never catch a squirrel, no matter how long she tried.

Summer turned into fall. When my sister and I went back to school, our absence fostered a closer friendship between our dog and cat.

One day, a terrible commotion arose from two doors away. A ruckus at the neighbor's house disturbed the peace in the neighborhood. Hisses, howls, and screeches of a catfight sounded through the walls of our house. I ran outside.

Did the fight involve Tasha? Sure enough, Tasha mixed it up with the neighbor's cat. Since she fared so poorly against the squirrel, I was sure she'd lose. I readied myself to help her. But from what I saw, Tasha was winning. Then, strangely, she quit fighting.

What was she doing? Tasha ran for dear life toward our house and into the backyard. When she reached the center of the yard she stopped, sat down with her back toward the other cat, and began to groom herself, as if nothing happened. I knew our cat was not exactly normal, but had she completely lost her mind? The other cat, now recovered from her initial surprise, quickly closed the gap between them. She sensed the opportunity to snatch victory from the jaws of defeat and grew brave — and foolish. The neighbor's cat decided to show Tasha who was boss of the block.

The cat jumped our fence and ran toward Tasha, who remained oblivious, her back turned to the advancing enemy. I rushed toward the sliding glass door to warn her, but realized I was not the only one watching with keen interest. As Sheba waited patiently, the neighbor's cat got closer and closer.

Sheba sprang into action. With her trademark low growl, used on Cole Parker, the shepherd sprang to her feet and took off in a dead run toward the feline intruder. The neighbor's cat froze for a split second. Surely, she felt at least three of her nine lives slip away. She realized she had been duped.

That cat retreated faster than any cat I've ever seen. Sheba's jaws snapped shut on empty air just an instant after the neighbor's cat leaped for safety, her hind feet just grazing the top of our fence into friendly territory. I'm sure I saw the cat's tail pass between Sheba's teeth like dental floss. Tasha watched the whole scene, apparently with great amusement. My cat and dog had worked as a team, setting up the neighbor's cat for an ambush, and almost pulled it off. The other cat never set a paw in Tasha's territory again.

The unlikely duo of Sheba and Tasha proved to be a lasting friendship we never thought possible. They taught me that the most unlikely of companions could sort out their own relationship, if given half a chance. Companion animals are often much more open-minded about differences than the humans around them.

Author's note to our readers sensitive to prevailing thought in animal welfare; this story took place in the late 1960's when no one we knew kept an indoor-only cat. With the rise of diseases like feline leukemia and feline

immunodeficiency virus (FIV), we now know that indoor cats live longer, healthier lives.

CHAPTER 2
MAGGIE DID IT TO HERSELF

When I graduated high school and moved away from home, my daily connection with animal rescue all but disappeared. I enjoyed my college days at the University of Georgia in Athens, but my only regular connection with an animal soul was with my girlfriend's rather anti-social cat, appropriately named Psycho. Those years dedicated to higher learning were an interesting mix of intellectual pursuits and social debauchery. Visits home were occasions to enjoy my mother's cooking and listen while she and my aunt recounted stories about the Humane Society animals I missed meeting. As much as I missed sharing my life with a dog, my early life experiences left me with a deep understanding of the commitment we owe our companion animals. I knew, without needing to hear it from my family, that I was not responsible enough to make that commitment yet.

A few years later, I met the woman with whom I wanted to spend my life. We married and started a family. I was (at least in theory) grown up, responsible and content. But our home was not complete. I knew what was missing. My wife felt it, too. It was time to make the commitment, to add a dog to our household. Never considering any other alternative, we looked up the location of the closest animal shelter. In the early 1990's animal rescue, advocates still struggled to gain attention and funding in the Atlanta area. Our drive to the Atlanta Humane Society's shelter took over an hour from our home in the northern suburbs. Our young son, an audacious toddler with a rapidly expanding vocabulary, accompanied us on the journey.

The Atlanta Humane Society caseworker introduced us to several nice dogs, but our son repeatedly returned to the same fluffy black-and-white ball of fur. "I want dat one," he said as he pointed his pudgy little finger.

The caseworker read from her obligatory folder of paperwork and dutifully informed us with a straight face that we were looking at a beagle puppy. I knew beagles. This was no beagle puppy. However, her dubious lineage was irrelevant to our son, whose mind was made up. And so we adopted Maggie the border collie. She was a wonderful dog, one who would be considered a "once in a lifetime" companion if we had not been destined to later share our lives with so many unique animals.

Unnervingly intelligent, loyal, and tolerant, Maggie Mae turned out to be the perfect addition to our young family. She remains the center of many childhood memories for our children. We made many mistakes as we learned to be responsible caregivers, but her trust, love, and resilience taught us the truth behind the Josh Billings quote, "A dog is the only thing on earth that loves you more than you love yourself." This story sheds a glimmer of light on Maggie's special place in our family.

The case started for me when this young dame by the name of Maggie sashayed demurely into my office. When I gave her the once over, she turned aside like she had something to hide. It piqued my curiosity, so I investigated, 'cause that's what I do. But I don't need no stinkin' badge.

Some joker messed her up pretty good. From her neck to her belly, Maggie was colored a bright, waxy red. She didn't have to say a word. Actually, she couldn't say a word. Maggie doesn't speak English, only canine.

Anger coursed through my veins. This gumshoe was on the job. Finding a suspect proved easy. I started in what I believed was the vicinity of the crime scene and walked the grid. Soon I came across primary suspect numero uno.

This young shifty-looking kid named Matt looked innocent, but he had guilt written all over his face. Well, actually, he had red lipstick all over his fingers. Not the same thing as a smoking gun, but it was good enough for me.

I encouraged him to spill the beans. "Go ahead, kid. Make it easy on yourself. Confess what you've done. I'll see the Judge goes easy on you."

The kid was tough; I had to hand that to him. But I'm tougher, and I had him red-handed. Well, at least red-fingered. I pointed out the obvious, but he stunned me by his answer: "Maggie did it to herself."

Such audacity! I had to admit the kid had thrown me for a loop, didn't see that one comin'. I went to confer with the boss, the Chief of Detectives, the head honcho. Sometimes, I call her Boss, but other times I call her Lisa. Or sweetie.

"Whaddya think?" I asked her.

"Beats me. You picked up the ball on this one. You run with it."

Okay, so the Chief wasn't going to be much help . I'm on my own. Maybe she knows something I don't, but she isn't talkin' any more than Maggie.

I took a second run at my suspect, trying to break down his alibi. "Okay, son, you said, 'Maggie did it to herself.'

But that story just isn't gonna hold water. Here's the problem. Dogs don't have opposable thumbs!"

I triumphantly towered over him. My size advantage intimidated him while I reveled in the brilliance of my logic. Surely the kid would crack under this pressure, especially after I'd just destroyed his alibi. Maggie didn't do it because she couldn't do it, see?

The kid didn't crack or even waver. He stared me down, uh, up, and repeated, "Maggie did it to herself."

He was no ordinary adversary. It became increasingly obvious; a confession would not be forthcoming. I thought it best to confer with the Judge. I didn't worry about warrants or any of that legal nonsense. I worried about crossing the Judge. Sometimes she lets me call her Lisa.

"Your honor, or sweetheart — I forget how the conversation started — this is one tough nut to crack. I need advice on how to move forward. The kid isn't confessin'."

Displaying the wisdom accorded her office, the Judge asked, "Do you have any witnesses?"

Of course, I knew from experience that Maggie wasn't gonna talk. I mean, if she did, we'd have to call Ripley's Believe It or Not, because she'd be the first dog ever to speak English. I returned to scour the neighborhood, or should I say, the other bedrooms — to find out if anyone else saw anything.

I looked for a snitch named Stephanie and got lucky, caught her in her room. "Did you see Matt color on Maggie?" I knew it was a leading question, and I led her right to the answer I wanted to hear. It didn't have to stand up in a court of law, but it would have to pass scrutiny by the Judge.

"Yes." Stephanie said with no preamble. So there. I had a corroborating witness.

Judge Lisa pointed out the potential for bias in my primary witness. After all, she was Matt's big sister. She'd sell him down the river for a half hour of phone privileges or a stack of Oreos. The judge had a point.

So I took one last shot at cracking the kid. "Son, this is your last chance. Tell the truth, and I'll put in a good word with Mom (the judge). I'll get your sentence suspended. But if you keep lying to me, I'm going to ask that she throw the book at you. I'm gonna recommend a… time out!"

I watched him visibly squirm at the threat, especially 'cause I was loud. Victory seemed within my grasp. The kid wasn't cut out for hard time. But to my surprise, he stubbornly held his ground and repeated, "Maggie did it to herself."

"Okay, kid, that's it. Get in that chair in the corner, and I mean right now, mister! You don't want me to get rough with you, do you? In the chair. Now!"

"Yes, sir." He sniffed back tears as he trudged to the corner, his shoulders slumped in defeat. I stormed out of the room, angry with myself because I failed to get his confession. Under the circumstances, I couldn't negotiate a more lenient sentence.

Chief of Detectives Lisa was conducting a follow up interview with Stephanie. I suspected the chief would soon accuse me of bias. After all, Judge Lisa knew all too well about Stephanie's rap sheet, which is longer than my arm. This is no household of angels we're talking about here.

"Hey, gumshoe, take a look at this."

Immediately I became suspicious, having the chief of detectives, a.k.a. judge, snooping around my case. After all, she was also the kid's mother. Maybe I was being set up as the fall guy.

When I stepped through the door and saw Lisa on her knees looking under the bed, a bad feeling settled in the pit of my stomach.

"Whatcha got, boss?" My interest interlaced with dread.

"I think there's something you've overlooked here that's gonna spring the kid." I got close to see for myself.

Sure enough, under the bed she found a telltale swath of red, about six inches long and four inches wide. I called Maggie. She slunk into the room with a guilty air, but I coaxed her with an encouraging tone of voice.

The eyeball test confirmed without a doubt, the red marks on Maggie's belly matched the smear on the carpet. The kid hadn't lied. Technically speaking, Maggie did it to herself.

Sure, he'd colored the carpet, but that wasn't the charge. He'd been accused of coloring the dog. She really colored herself as she crawled under Stephanie's bed to hide.

I shook my head in disgust. My bungling allowed a criminal mastermind to walk away, scot-free, despite his obvious guilt. No choice. I had to cut him loose. The judge was in no mood for me to charge the perp with a different count for the same basic offense. She's let me know in no uncertain terms — that would constitute double jeopardy.

So the kid walked, time served.

CHAPTER 3
BELLE

After proving ourselves capable of providing more than adequate care for both Maggie Mae and her grandchildren, my mother itched to get us into more involved with rescue work. Surely, our home was incomplete with only one dog. The very idea that anyone in our extended family could fail to open their hearts and hearths to several dogs in need was simply scandalous. My sister already had two dogs and three cats, so I was falling miserably behind my mother's expectations.

Belle the Dalmatian joined our family for the remaining years of our children's youth and beyond. She was still with us during the peak of our fostering years. A simple-minded, undemanding, and affectionate dog, Belle could easily blend into the background. She usually played the good-natured supporting role to the brightest stars in our canine pack.

Belle taught us there are many reasons people backpedal on keeping an animal once they make the commitment. Had she not ended up with us, her life likely held one episode after another of being surrendered to a shelter. Mild-mannered Belle carried a silent but deadly secret.

When he was almost three years old, our son Matt's favorite movie was the Disney animated feature 101 Dalmatians. Like many children his age, he was obsessed with the handsome breed of spotted dogs. The wide commercial success of the movie meant every preschooler asked his or her parents, grandparents, and Santa Claus for a polka-dotted puppy. For several years, irresponsible over-breeding led to an abundance of Dalmatians housed in animal shelters across the country. In a story repeated all too often, two young roommates in Savannah inspired by the movie purchased an adorable purebred Dalmatian puppy. Once the novelty of sporting around town with the miniature movie star wore off, they surrendered her to the animal shelter, claiming a lack of time to spend with her.

As a regular volunteer, my mother saw many dogs as they arrived at the shelter. She fell in love when she met Lindy, a six-month-old purebred Dalmatian. Though she was registered and had her papers, the Humane Society spayed Lindy according to their policy, to prevent adding to the overbreeding problem. Knowing our son's fascination with the breed, my mother saw the perfect opportunity to save a life, endear herself eternally to her young grandson, and add to our woefully underutilized household with only a single dog. The puppy's plight coincided with Matt's upcoming birthday. Mom was sure it must be destiny. Over the years, Mom reminded me on a number of occasions that she did actually phone ahead to ask our permission before bringing Lindy to our home. Years later, our recollection of actually agreeing to adopt Belle became a bit fuzzy in the haze of hindsight.

We already had Maggie, the black-and-white border collie that metamorphosed from a beagle puppy. She was past the high maintenance puppy months, completely house trained and no longer chewing on everything in sight.

Mom promised that Lindy was housetrained. I rationalized that Maggie would enjoy Lindy's company while we were at work during the day, so we accepted Mom's offer.

Matt squealed with delight the next weekend when Grandma climbed out of her car in our driveway with the perfect miniature replica of his favorite movie character, Pongo. He loved Lindy at first sight. We did have one problem, though. Matt had difficulty saying her name, at only three years of age. I suggested we choose a name for her from his favorite movie. He liked Pongo, despite my reminder that Pongo was the daddy dog in the movie, and Lindy was a girl. As the most logical alternative, I suggested Purdie, the mother dog's name.

Matt wanted no part of it. I tried to rationalize with a three-year-old while I stubbornly refused to give the female dog a masculine name, but Matt didn't like my other suggestions from the Dalmatians movie. Luckily, Disney made several other wonderful cartoon films around the same time, so after the family unanimously shot down naming Lindy after Ariel from The Little Mermaid, we all agreed on Belle, the heroine from Beauty and the Beast. The double-entendre of the feminine character name, combined with the Dalmatian breed's stereotypical association with fire stations, which use bells and sirens to alert the community, made the name seem a perfect fit.

That might have seemed, at least from a distance, the missing piece to complete the perfect family. We were two parents, a Mom and a Dad; two children, a boy and a girl; and now two handsome black-and-white canines.

During the normal weeks of adjusting to a new home, Belle became fast friends with Maggie. She willingly fell into the role of amiable sidekick, following her brilliant older canine role model around in unabashed awe. Belle basked in Matt's love and thrived under Maggie's tutelage.

By routine, our happy family gathered to watch television in the family room after dinner. One night, during a commercial break, we heard the rather loud and unmistakable sound of flatulence break the silence of the moment. Our oldest child, Stephanie, sprung up from her spot on the floor beside Belle. With her characteristic adolescent flair for the dramatic, she pointed accusingly toward the dog. "Gross, it's Belle. She is — like — lethal."

Poor, naive Belle flicked her eyes quickly around the room, wondering what she'd done wrong. She sensed she had committed some egregious offense, but was clueless as to what it might be. She shot a pleading glance at Maggie, hoping for guidance. Maggie ventured to the other side of the room, leaving no mistake as to whom to blame.

So began our fourteen years of living with Belle's one real fault. It turned out that Belle was cursed with gastro-intestinal issues that would plague her throughout her life. In short order, we learned to carefully regulate her diet or else be prepared for inhaling toxic fumes.

Belle was extraordinarily sweet, and as Matt often said, "She is my dog and she yuvs me." She was a very gentle dog, never dreaming of challenging Maggie for the dominant role. But Belle was not exactly defenseless. She could produce weapons of mass destruction, capable of waking a person from a sound sleep in the middle of the night. We only knew that because she did, more than once.

On a day I will never forget, I collapsed in a heap on our bed after arriving home from work. I threw myself face down, feeling like an exhausted lump of human flesh, my arms flopped out to each side, and my chin hooked over the edge on the bed. I closed my eyes and drifted near sleep. Maggie came up, nuzzled my dangling hand in gentle greeting, and accepted my affectionate scratching behind her ears, doled out without bothering to open my eyes. I could tell one dog from the other by their coats — Maggie was longhaired, while Belle's fur formed short, wire-like bristles. Once she was satisfied, Maggie wandered off to find the kids. Belle waited her turn, and then tried to follow Maggie's example in order to receive fair share of attention.

Belle began at one end of the bed and walked along the perimeter, rubbing her body against the bed skirt as she approached me. As she ambled around, she emitted a silent but deadly sustained explosion of gas that spread over the bed like a cloud of napalm, completely permeating the room. I began to gag on the fumes about the same time Belle reached my head. My eyes snapped open as quickly as if someone had shoved smelling salts under my nose. Except this smell was much worse than ammonia.

I fled my bedroom, with Belle in hot pursuit. She didn't understand that I was running away from her; she only knew that she still hadn't received her share of my affection. I had bailed out before giving her love. The overpowering scent left me no choice.

But she was so guileless, so unaffected in her love for me, and looked so pitiful with her head drooping and tail wagging uncertainly as I walked away...my heart took precedence over my nose. I stopped and turned around.

"Come on, girl," I motioned to Belle as I walked to the back door and waited to lead her out onto the deck, where I gratefully sucked fresh air into my lungs.

I would swear she smiled as I bent down to scratch her ears.

CHAPTER 4
THE MIGHTY OX

Our children grew toward their teenage years and gradually needed less of our time. It was a bittersweet time, watching our children make their own way in the world. I felt satisfied and content, seeing their depth of compassion for their fellow beings. To this day, both Stephanie and Matt sense the impact their actions have on those around them and are sensitive to the feelings of others, perhaps more so than most of their peers. I attribute this, at least partially, to raising them with respect for the most helpless among us — companion animals that rely on us for sustenance and care.

After adopting Belle, we continued to help lost dogs along the way. Lisa and I worked hard to learn dog training and behavior modification skills. We discovered we both had a knack for it — an almost intuitive ability to calm a frightened dog, gain a confused animal's trust, and defuse potentially dangerous situations. Ever the researcher, Lisa found training techniques she shared with me regularly.

During these years, we added a puppy named Sheba to our household, accepting her from one of our daughter's young friends who was ill equipped to care for herself, let alone an animal. Sheba II grew into the most perfect German Shepherd Dog ever to live, the greatest dog ever. Period. I will always cherish fond memories of the massive but gentle giant reaching out with gargantuan paw to "stiff arm" an obnoxious puppy wearing on her last nerve.

Sheba's remarkable life and its lasting impact on our own were cut short by a rare and previously incurable disease. She was one the first dogs in the world to undergo an experimental treatment for systemic aspergillosis. Though the infection stopped for a while, it had gotten into her bones. Her story is still too painful to tell. But this is the appropriate place in our journey to acknowledge her life, and the impact she had on us. She inspired us to be better people. While she was with us, she taught us how to foster, heal, and rehabilitate broken dogs that came through our home.

Sheba, your life was not in vain. What you taught us led us to save many lives in your honor. Rest well, beloved friend.

Meanwhile, our home became the one in the neighborhood others knew to bring stray or hurt animals. Our efforts were still at the individual level. We were not yet involved in the daily struggle of life and death that would characterize our later dedication to animal rescue. One such experience that prepared us for the fight and strengthened our conviction is recounted here.

Ox was a rescue that preceded, and perhaps precipitated, our work with the Humane Society. The inspiration for the character of the same name in my Robert Mercer mystery novel Coastal Empire, the real-life Ox is not nearly so well trained. However, he is equally if not even more faithful to me than his fictional counterpart is to

Mercer. The real-life Ox would run through a brick wall for me. I have told my wife many times that I wish she loved me as much as Ox.

The people renting one of my houses asked permission to keep a dog in the backyard. I pointed out the obvious — the yard had no fence.

"Oh, I can keep him on a run," Rick, my tenant, said. We stood in the driveway of the modest home, looking into the sloped backyard. It was a large yard, grass growing in some areas and others covered in leaves and pine straw. A few trees dotted the back property line, providing some sparse shade.

He and his wife Veronica introduced me to the large, solid black German Shepherd Dog sitting patiently behind them.

"What's his name?" I offered my hand for the dog to sniff as Rick held him on an improvised leash of yellow nylon cord.

Rick grinned apologetically. "We rescued him from a couple of meth heads who kept him tied to a tree. They called him Oxy, short for Oxycontin."

I shook my head in disbelief.

"It's really a shame that he's dying," he added, rubbing the dog behind one ear as he spoke.

"What? He doesn't even look sick!"

"Our vet says he has heartworms, but the treatments are too expensive and it's too late to help him," Veronica volunteered. She avoided looking at the dog. I got the impression Oxy was here by Rick's choice, not hers.

"I think you need a new vet," I snorted in disgust.

Once I reached home, I called the expert for her opinion — my mother. "Hey, Mom… I've got a couple of tenants with a dog that has heartworms. They said their vet told them it's too late to save the dog. I know y'all have had to deal with heartworms at the Humane Society before. How late is too late? He's a nice dog and he's still young, not more than a couple of years old."

"Is he coughing? Having difficulty breathing?"

"No…he doesn't even look sick."

"Then he's probably still in stage one. There are five stages of heartworm disease. I've seen dogs that were coughing up blood that survived heartworm treatment. The dog you are describing is still easily treated and cured at that stage. It is expensive, though. Maybe the real problem is that your tenants can't afford the treatment."

"It's possible. Thanks, Mom."

Our conversation left me with plenty to think about. The image of the black dog nagged at my conscience that night.

My own dog, Belle, was due at our vet for a round of vaccines, so I broached the subject of heartworm treatment with Dr. Andy.

"I have a couple of tenants with a large German Shepherd Dog that has heartworms. Their regular vet told them the dog couldn't be saved, but I've seen him, and from what I learned so far about heartworms, I think he's still in stage one. I think the real problem might be they can't afford the treatment. If they brought the dog to you, would you be willing to treat him if I guaranteed they will pay the bill and agreed to cover any expenses they don't pay? Could you break the cost of the treatment down into payments for them?"

We had been clients of Dr. Andy's for a number of years and had a good relationship. I knew he was a good and compassionate veterinarian. I was not disappointed by his response. He readily agreed to an installment payment plan and told me to have them call the office for an appointment.

Oxy underwent treatment over a six-week period, and Dr. Andy declared him cured. On my next visit to the house, he greeted me with a mournful wail, desperate for attention on his run. Rick had secured a steel cable between two trees about thirty yards apart, and attached Oxy to a lead on a rolling pulley. It gave the dog a decent amount of room to run, but he lacked freedom and companionship.

"I thought once he started the heartworm treatment, you'd keep him in the house. You know how bad it would be for him to contract heartworms a second time, don't you?" I asked Rick. He avoided eye contact and muttered an excuse about one of his children having allergies.

How many landlords argue with their tenants to keep the dog in the house rather than outside? I asked myself. As Rick and Veronica scurried inside the house and out several times during my visit, I learned the truth.

Ahhh... the reason Oxy can't stay in the house is because they have a little yippy dog and two cats they never mentioned.

They may have meant well when they took in Oxy, but I began to have trust issues with Rick and Veronica.

It wasn't the dog's fault these people wouldn't let him stay in the house. Then I began to worry when reports of coyote attacks circulated through the neighborhood. I envisioned a helpless dog trapped on a lead, as a pack of vicious wild animals circled him, biding their time.

So, I paid a contractor to fence in the backyard for Oxy.

"Are you crazy?" my wife asked. I assumed the question was rhetorical.

On my next visit to collect the rent, Oxy seemed to enjoy his new yard and freedom from the lead wire. As far as I knew, it was the first time in his life he had not been tied to something. He made a lot of racket. I couldn't tell if he was being territorial or starved for attention. I cracked the gate open just enough to pass the dog a Milk-Bone as a token of peace. He didn't take it from my hand, so I dropped it on the ground and withdrew, closing the gate with a feeling of pity. Although Rick and Veronica took decent care of him, the dog obviously craved the inclusion of his pack.

The following month, Veronica was involved in a very serious car accident. Rear-ended by a teenager on his cell phone, she suffered severe back injuries. Rick assumed the role of primary caregiver. They were both spending long periods away from home. She was hospitalized for a week, and then moved on to intensive physical therapy.

I found myself dropping by the house more often, trying to help with the small maintenance tasks while Rick was overwhelmed with Victoria's care. Oxy barked and howled when I visited, making me wonder if he was protective of his yard or anxious with loneliness. On every visit, I spoke to him through the privacy fence I constructed in his honor, unsure of his intentions. Eventually, I opened the gate and let myself into the backyard, careful that he didn't escape. I extended the webbed face of a tennis racquet as a shield to keep him at bay until I got the gate closed firmly behind me.

The sound he made next tore at my heart — a plaintive, keening wail with a hint of pent-up frustration. He desperately wanted to get close to me. But why — to lick me or bite me? My tennis racquet still separated us. My other hand held a now-familiar peace token, a Milk-Bone.

It occurred to me that I should use his name as often as possible. He might not remember me, but I wanted him to know that I knew his name.

"Oxy, do you want a treat?"

He gingerly took the treat from my outstretched hand. When I finally lowered the racquet, he dropped his Milk-Bone and rushed to my side. He plopped to the ground with a thud like a bag of cement. The poor dog was practically begging me to pet him.

He's starving for attention. Poor fella.

I felt sorry for the dog and for my tenants. They weren't at fault in the accident — Veronica had been hit hard, injuring both her back and neck. Rick was trying to run his business, care for Veronica, and keep their two children in school.

Fortunately, I didn't live very far from the house, so I continued to keep an eye on Oxy while the woman continued her recovery. But a swift recovery was not in the cards. Her rehabilitation dragged on interminably. Rent payments were slower in coming. I forgave a month of unpaid rent out of sympathy for their situation.

Oxy began to anticipate my visits. I was no longer hesitant at the gate. I knew as soon as I stepped through, he would run up to me, drop to the ground, and roll over in submission. It was the heat of summer. The big black dog was in a yard without much shade. I noticed his water dish was very low, a film of algae beginning to develop. I washed it out and filled it.

Two days later the entire family was gone when I arrived at the house around noon. His water dish was empty again. I wondered how long it had been empty, whether anyone even checked on it since I was there last. I called my wife and explained the situation.

"What do you think I should do?" I asked her. "I hate giving Rick and Veronica grief when they are going through such a hard time, but I can't stand to watch a dog suffer from neglect, either."

"Other than the problem with the water, does he look healthy? Has he been eating?" she asked.

"Well, he's not as fat as our dog, if that's what you mean. Overall, he looks healthy, except one of his eyes has gunk crusted on it. I'm also worried about heartworms. If they're having difficulty remembering to keep his water bowl filled, they might not be giving him his heartworm preventive, either."

"What's wrong with his eye? What color is the discharge?"

"It looks yellowish."

My wife sighed. "You'd better run him to the vet and get the eye checked out."

Fifty bucks later, I had eye medicine. Rather than return him to his yard, I knew I needed to bring Oxy home with me. I called Rick, leaving him a message to explain why I had taken his dog, and then phoned Lisa to prepare her for our houseguest.

Her voice on the other end of the phone was pensive. She felt concern for Oxy's situation, but weighed the practicalities of bringing him into our house. "You know you're taking a big chance, don't you? What if he doesn't get along with Sheba? She hasn't been challenged by another dog her size before. If he hasn't been eating regularly, he might be food aggressive. How are you going to handle it?"

"Honey, you're the one who watches The Dog Whisperer every week. What would Cesar do? He'd keep his tennis racquet handy in case he needed to separate the dogs without being bitten. Get a water spray bottle ready, just in case. Everything will be fine," I said with false bravado. I had no idea what I was doing.

Sheba was our existing canine family member, a large female black-and-tan German Shepherd Dog — a classic beauty, as regal as she was intelligent. She sized up Oxy in the first few minutes and decided he was a dog of good character. She and Oxy quickly became friendly companions. Thankfully, Oxy never showed the first sign of any food aggression. He ate what he wanted, then watched in idle fascination as Sheba came after him to finish anything he left in his dish.

His house manners were another story, though. Oxy was like a bull in a china shop. He careened around the house, barking for attention. He knocked over vases and stepped on toes. In attempts to communicate his excitement, he scraped his large paws over our arms or legs. His exuberant joy of being indoors, of having companionship and interaction with other beings was a bit overwhelming for us at first.

I worked on discipline. I got two treats out and gave commands.

"Sheba, sit!" She dutifully sat and received her treat.

"Oxy. Sit," He offered to shake hands, putting his paw out. "No, sit!" I repeated. Frustrated, he dropped to the ground as if he'd been shot with a fast acting tranquilizer dart. I could not help laughing. "Close enough," I said as I handed over the treat.

At first Oxy intimidated my wife a little because of his size and unruly behavior. However, her heart melted when she saw how fiercely devoted he became to us in a very short period. He bonded most closely with me, identifying me as his rescuer. He was intent on repaying the debt by never leaving my side, on constant vigil for any harm that might befall me, ever alert for my every move.

"What are you going to do when it's time to return Oxy to your tenants?" my wife asked a week later, stroking Oxy's back as we all piled onto the couch.

"We'll cross that bridge when we come to it," I hedged. I knew even then I could never part with the dog that looked to us now as his family, the pack he so desperately needed.

Finally, I spoke with Rick by phone. He was home for a few moments between business calls, after visiting with Veronica in the hospital. He wearily agreed that Oxy should stay with me while his eye needed treatment. I bragged, "And when you get him back, there won't be any reason to keep him in the backyard anymore. He will be fully housetrained by the time he comes back home to you."

Rick sounded non-committal about the idea.

What am I going to do if he wants Oxy back?

As days passed, Oxy calmed down, becoming more relaxed around the house. It still broke my heart to see him guard the water dish. The dog remembered those scorching days when the temperatures rose near 100 degrees and water became such a precious commodity for him. Even with constant access to water bowls now, he still chose a spot near the water whenever he curled up to rest. Upon waking, he invariably walked over to the water bowls with a haunting need to reassure himself it was still not empty.

I knew I could not manufacture reasons to delay returning Oxy to Rick and Veronica after his eye infection treatment was completed. But it would be very bad, and very unnecessary, if Oxy were to contract heartworms again for simple lack of prevention.

The clock kept ticking.

I discovered that Oxy loved riding shotgun in the van with me. All I had to do was open the minivan side door with the remote control, then open the front door of our house. Oxy would shoot out of our house like a black bullet. Slower to react than Oxy, Sheba found herself relegated to the bench seat behind us. She was a bit miffed to lose her favorite spot, but was much too dignified to tussle over it.

Slowing down with age now, Belle our Dalmatian was content to watch Oxy and Sheba entertain each other. She preferred long naps in the warm sun to chasing a tennis ball or tug-of-war. Oxy was careful around her, sensing that her elderly joints were sensitive to being jostled.

The two dogs had become practically inseparable. Oxy and Sheba became two bookends occupying either end of the couch. A very determined human being could squeeze in between them, as long as it was someone who wasn't bothered by a little dog hair.

I remember the day I first noticed their synchronized window silhouettes. A squirrel ran across deck outside the glass doors of our family room. I watched in amazement at how they both sat in rapt attention, looking out the back window, their heads turning in tandem like poetry, even their ears cocked at the same angle and noses tilted to the identical degree. Oxy was the perfect complement to the regal "Queen Sheba."

He had become a fixture in our house. Yet his status officially remained unchanged. Rick and Veronica had begun struggling to pay their mounting bills, not to mention the rent. They seemed to be avoiding me as a result. My apprehensions grew as every day passed, while Oxy's status remained up in the air. Finally, Rick called me again.

"We've been thinking and talking about it, and with my wife's condition what it is, it would probably be best if you just kept Oxy… assuming you'd like to keep him."

His words were music to my ears. I couldn't accept his offer fast enough. But first, I needed to get my wife's approval. That wasn't as hard as I anticipated. Lisa was attached to Oxy now, too. She said, "Okay, but on one condition. We have got to change his name. I feel funny having a dog named after an illicit drug."

Her request was simple enough and made sense. However, Oxy had grown accustomed to his name. One of my favorite bands was The Who. I thought about their bass player. "Why don't we just shorten his name to Ox? We can explain that he's been named in honor of John

Entwistle because his nickname is The Ox. I think it would confuse the dog to give him a drastically different name."

Never a big Who fan, she reluctantly agreed.

The Mighty Ox settled into our household.

That uncomfortable call came about a month later. Out of the blue, Rick asked, "Could you bring Oxy over to the house so that we can say goodbye? We never got to see him again after he came down with that eye infection."

How can I say no? What if Ox wants to stay with them?

"Do you think he'd be okay riding over here in the car?" Rick asked. I laughed silently at the thought. One of the easiest things in the world to do was to get Ox to go for a ride.

"They're going to want to keep him," my wife worried. She offered up a few reasons I might use for delaying the visit.

But Ox had been their dog. They had originally rescued him and had been decent caregivers, up to the point where recovery from personal injury consumed their lives.

I leashed Ox this time as we left the house instead of letting him run headlong into the van. He sensed this outing was not our usual routine. Sheba stayed behind, whining and pacing. Ox took his place in the passenger's seat and looked at me with trusting eyes. I pulled out of our driveway, wondering if this was my last drive with the big black dog that was so much a part of our family now.

Ox grew apprehensive as we approached the rental house. He knew where he was, but not why he was there. Perhaps he was afraid he would have to stay there, returned to the backyard where he spent so many lonely hours and thirsty days. I got out of the van and pulled gently on his leather leash. Reluctantly, he followed me to the front porch.

My tenants scrambled over each other in their rush outside to greet him. But for Ox, the homecoming was very subdued.

On the way over, I had worried that he might become too exuberant to see his old family and inadvertently hurt Veronica in her fragile condition, still suffering in her effort to recover. My concern was for naught.

Ox was polite, but he only left my side reluctantly and greeted them timidly. As soon as he surmised he had met his obligation, my dog returned to his place by my side. His actions were unmistakable, his goodbye final. Rick and Veronica thanked me politely for bringing him over.

Using the remote control, I opened the door of the van and dropped his leash. Ox shot like a rocket for the car and assumed his favorite spot in the passenger's seat. He never looked back.

CHAPTER 5
HAIR TRIGGER

Shortly after we brought Ox into our family, my wife became serious about finding a local rescue organization with a philosophy and mission aligned with ours. She convinced me that we could make a bigger difference in the lives of animals if we joined forces with like-minded people. The introduction to this book chronicles her involvement and dedication to the neighboring county's Humane Society.

After a few successful placements of foster dogs we took in as responders to the desperate emails begging for help, Lisa felt drawn to help some of the long-term shelter dogs.

Trigger was our first "challenging" foster. A long-term resident of the shelter, we were afraid Trigger have become so institutionalized that he may never crave human interaction again. Trigger taught us about the resilience of a dog's soul, the undeniable thirst for pack acceptance, and the truth to our motto, "There is a perfect home for every dog, some just take a bit longer to find than others." He found his perfect home and still loves life there with his beagle buddy, Betsy.

My wife Lisa abounds with compassion and energy. Both of our lives changed forever, the day she volunteered with our local Humane Society. Wanting me to experience the same joy she received from helping at the shelter, she drafted me into service. She brought a dog home for us to foster.

There is a method to the madness of running a non-profit (and non-government) animal shelter with a skeleton crew of paid staff and a complement of dedicated volunteers. Dogs deemed highly adoptable are kept at the shelter for maximum exposure to visitors, people searching the kennels for their ideal animal companion. Dogs that required special care and any overflow of strays are farmed out to foster homes.

Fostering dogs includes an inherent danger. We human beings tend to fall in love and want to keep them all. When we started fostering animals, we maintained a respectable average; three dogs lived in our house. Today we have six...or seven, if Lisa comes home with a dog tonight. But she'll probably arrive empty handed, because she brought home a kitten yesterday.

My wife left to pick up a dog from the vet's office and drop it off at another foster home. If something happened at her destination, the dog would come back home with her. As the years passed, we became the contingency Plan B for many foster dogs in need.

We soon realized that our home was ideally suited for fostering multiple dogs. Set back from the street on one of the larger lots in the small subdivision, a long driveway led past a fishpond and expansive front lawn, up a hill to our single story ranch style house. French doors opened from every room across the back of the house, making it easy to control which dogs went outside together. A large wooden deck and screened porch provided room for sun-warmed naps to several canines, even stretched out to their full lengths. Our back yard was wooded and fenced. The rear property line was much longer than the front, creating a long, wide back yard perfect for running at full speed from one end to the other. A quiet pasture lay beyond the back fence. Our home was far from traffic dangers and it was the rare door-to-door solicitor ambitious enough to make the long walk up our driveway to ring the doorbell.

Among the first dogs Lisa brought home in our early fostering days was Trigger. He proved the easiest-going dog I'd ever met. If any single word best described this dog, it must be unflappable. No matter how excited or agitated the other dogs in our home became, Trigger seemed happy and grateful to be with us.

Trigger looked an overgrown beagle at first sight. Lisa described his breed as a Treeing Walker Coonhound — Trigger was actually purebred. Like all the dogs at the animal shelter, he no longer needed papers. Once neutered, an animal's credentials became largely irrelevant. Of course, all shelter animals are spayed or neutered prior to their adoption, helping to reverse the trend rather than add to the plethora of unwanted animals.

Otherwise a beautiful dog, Trigger had an opaque film clouding his left eye, suggesting blindness or an earlier injury. This made him less adoptable. In his previous home, Trigger had been stuck in a yard on a chain for long periods. Given adequate food and water, he endured a lonely, solitary life with little love and attention. Trigger had some rough edges. Because of his eye condition, Lisa and I debated whether the eye should be removed. The vet said the blind eye didn't appear to bother Trigger and there was no infection, so we decided against needless surgery.

Trigger grew up a yard dog because he had never been properly house trained. Wanting a better life for him in the future, we committed to teaching him house manners. From the moment he arrived in our home, Trigger sought to mark territory for himself, lifting his leg at every opportunity, as untrained male dogs do. He succeeded the first few times.

After using half a roll of paper towels, Lisa and I introduced Trigger to our backyard. We devised a strategy to save our furniture and walls from territorial marking. Quoting Barney Fife, "You've got to nip it in the bud." We knew we had to housebreak this dog, or he would never be appealing to a good home. Lisa researched the problem and found how to design a bellyband.

Think of a bellyband as a rectangular diaper for a male dog. Although commercially manufactured models are available, it is easy enough to cut a long strip of absorbent material like a towel. Wrap the band underneath the dog, covering his male parts, then tie or pin the ends over the dog's back.

The bellyband, after the dog had his accident, soon became a urine-soaked irritant held close to his body, making him uncomfortable. Wearing the bellyband soon taught Trigger proper indoor etiquette inside the house and protected our furniture during the training. Lisa also figured out, if she tied the contraption just right, the dog would lift his leg and wet himself instead of the spot he wanted. Trigger learned to stand by the back door for us to remove the band and go outside.

Problem solved.

It took time for Trigger to acclimate to indoor life. We turned on the television; it was our misfortune a music video that aired frightened him into a corner. Any loud unexpected noises, like the doorbell or the phone, startled

Trigger for a few days, but he settled into a calmer routine within a week.

My fondest memory is when Trigger learned how to curl into the tightest ball possible and fall asleep in our bed, right between my wife and me. Once he wriggled into position, Trigger literally became an organic space heater. He learned to love human companionship, but enjoyed running with our dog pack.

Once we house trained Trigger, his popularity in our home soared. Our previous foster dogs had only been with us a week or two before someone found their stories and photographs online. We had sort of a revolving doggie-door for foster dogs. Trigger became our first houseguest to stay for an extended period. But he also made a distinct impression on some neighbors who were causing us problems.

I vividly remember how Trigger acted toward a horse pastured on our property line. Two white horses and a red one grazed in that field during the fall months. The white mares had reasonably good manners, but Red Horse sought a bit of mischief.

He grazed right next to the fence at every opportunity, as if grass there tasted better than anywhere else in his pasture. His nonchalant manner of eating grass plucked from the very base of our fence drove my dogs insane. Our German Shepherd Dogs were rather territorial and took offense at their cavalier flaunting from Red Horse.

Intrigued by their response, Red Horse escalated. He drew the shepherds to the fence by ignoring them, then pawed, snorted, and reared up. Red galloped up and down the fence line, seemingly intent on provoking the pack into a barking frenzy. My bad black shepherd, Ox, once got so upset, he finally broke a hole through the fence wire and charged the horses, chasing the three into an adjacent field. He retreated, guarding our property past the fence hole until

I discovered him on the wrong side. I repaired the fence break, Red Horse regained his confidence, and the whole scene repeated on a regular basis.

I liked the horses but wanted to do something to encourage Red Horse to graze away from our fence line. Ox received numerous cuts and scrapes in his battles with the fence. Clapping my hands and shooing Red away did little good. He resisted the intimidation of squirt guns full of water and shaker cans full of beans, showing little respect for me or my dogs.

Lisa and I planned to erect a six-foot wooden privacy fence between the dogs and the horses, the only solution we could think of to end the frustration. As I installed the first post, Trigger found his own unique solution. Red Horse pretended to graze right at the fence line, snorting at Ox, an invitation for the shepherd to come at him. The horse's attention focused on Ox, so he never noticed as Trigger approached.

Now Trigger had never shown the slightest interest in the horses. He approached, hiked his leg, and delivered a stream with pinpoint accuracy, a bull's eye to the middle of Red Horse's head. That got Red's undivided attention; he backed up and snorted all his objections from a safe distance. Red Horse learned the hard way that Trigger didn't need to get through the fence to reach him. And the once proud horse never again approached the fence for lunch.

Trigger proved quick on the draw, able to take dead aim. We had a new sheriff in town.

CHAPTER 6
AMAZING GRACIE

The impact of working with a rescue group lies in synergy — the ability to respond collectively to any given risk situation. Only a year into our involvement with the Humane Society, my heart went out to the dog in the latest email plea.

The lesson we learned in this story — information communicated in urgent email pleas for help by well-meaning volunteers is usually only about 20% accurate, at best. Why? Because there are many good-hearted people in the rescue world who, for whatever self-imposed reasons, decide they cannot help directly by providing shelter for one more animal in a garage or basement, not even for one single day. These well-meaning people salve their own consciences by inundating the rest of us — the doers — with sad, desperate stories on a daily basis

Then they fret over the lack of response to their pleas by "others." Alas, does no one care?

Speaking on behalf of the doers, "Yes, we care. Without our action, there would be no hope. Thank you for sending your email plea, but if I respond to your email instead of sticking with my plan to visit the local county shelter today and pull two dogs, how is that helpful? I saved the one life for which you pled, but perhaps two will be lost as a result. Am I not just sacrificing the life of the dog that was not lucky enough to be featured in your email — being compelled instead to drive three counties away to pull the one you decided was deserving of salvation? Your implication is that if I do not save this dog you are highlighting, I am not doing my part."

Now, let me get off my soapbox and say thanks, because at least you cared enough to send the email. It's a start. But allow me to speak for all of us with considerably more animals under our roofs tonight than would be considered comfortable, "Next time, please consider finding a way to get past your own perceived limitations, get off your keyboard and go pull the dog/cat yourself."

Those complaints now voiced, I am eternally grateful I responded to this particular email. I love this little girl. She is still my sunshine.

Hungry and hurt, the scared little grey dog shivered. No one knew for sure how long she'd been running loose near the busy intersection in John's Creek …at least two weeks, according to those who tried to catch her. How had she had survived so long without being killed? Statistics estimate 10,000 cars pass through that one busy intersection every day, near the bank the dog called home. She managed to evade death this long, nothing short of a miracle, as she continued her insane game of dodging cars on the street. Somehow, she eluded death and her capture.

Some of her pursuers suggested the dog was feral. She showed no trust of human beings. One thought the creature was part wolf, coyote, or some other wild animal. Given her relatively small size and markings, a few people wondered if she could be a lost German Shepherd puppy. Guessing was close as anyone got. Even the most experienced dog handlers could not get near the dog.

The stray was injured; an angry red streak on her hind leg indicated she suffered from an ugly open wound. She needed medical attention, if someone could capture her.

The branch manager at the bank had enticed the dog to come near, using food and treats. Over a few days, the dog developed a modicum of trust for the manager and made a hedge of shrubbery on the bank property her home base. Nevertheless, she shied away from human contact and foiled every effort to trap her. She accepted food from people, but nothing else.

The ranks of the volunteers trying to catch the evasive little dog swelled as others learned of her plight and wanted to save her from harm. But this dog was too smart and too quick. The group persisted, more desperate and determined than ever to succeed.

Recruited by email, my wife and I were enthusiastic to join the hunt for the canine artful dodger. Lisa received a hot tip where the dog hid herself, on the bank grounds. Like police racing in response to an emergency, we sped off to the rescue, dog treats and rope leads in hand.

That morning Suzanne, another pursuer of the dog, went to the bank with a dual purpose. Suzanne had noticed the dog running loose on a previous visit and tried to catch her. She was determined and proved little more creative than the rest of us. Scrolling through the contact names in her cell phone, Suzanne called friends she knew would help. She was unaware that Lisa and I were already among the volunteers from the local Humane Society, organized and working to save the dog. Lisa was one of the ringleaders, a primary conspirator in the effort to catch the stray, so when Suzanne called, Lisa updated her. We had now improved our odds of success.

The dog remained hidden in the hedge less than ten feet from Suzanne as we arrived that morning. Suzanne knew that cats communicate peace with a slow blink. It's their own sign meant to put other felines at ease. She blinked slowly at the dog and she spoke gently to her. The sweet words turned into a calming lilt, and then into song. The dog apparently loved listening to her sing. Suzanne softly sang every song that came to mind, bringing some peace to the distrustful animal. She coaxed the animal almost within arm's reach. The dog stayed there for two hours in a cold steady drizzle.

Lisa parked our minivan. She slipped out the driver's door and pushed it closed with little noise, not to startle the stray. Lisa dropped to the ground and crawled toward Suzanne; I followed her example. When Lisa asked me if I could identify the dog's breed, I rose from my crouch and got a better look. I locked eyes on the dog's glare as she watched me. Her ears flattened out and flexed downward on the sides of her head like TV antennae adjusted for better reception. And then she disappeared into the evening gloom; a flash of grey sped away and disappeared into the night. Yes, I felt like a complete idiot. Suzanne just spent two hours in cold, damp, and miserable weather, working diligently to gain the dog's trust — and I ruined it in 30 seconds.

For the next several hours, I walked around nearby businesses in the cold misting rain. I was miserable. I'd blown the best chance we had to bring this little stray to safety. In vain, I called out to the dog without a name. "Come here, baby. Sweetie, I won't hurt you. Here, baby." I searched under bushes, behind trashcans, and anywhere else I could imagine she might hide. She was long gone.

I remained distraught as we headed home, convinced someone would soon send out an email to announce that she'd been killed by a car. It would be my fault. The agony stayed with me for another two weeks. I visualized streams of traffic passing through that intersection, never seeming to thin much, no matter the time of day. I would stop often and search the area, mindful that the clock ticked against the little grey dog's luck, and I feared it would soon run out.

One day I would fret when no new sightings of the dog were reported. The next day I marveled more time passed without receiving news of her death. Every day was a new ride on my roller coaster of emotions.

Two more weeks elapsed. People still sighted the dog running loose in the same vicinity. Those two weeks seemed an eternity. Then Lisa called me on my cell phone from her office. Breathless with excitement she told me someone finally caught the dog and wondered if I could go pick her up and take her to the vet. I grabbed my car keys and headed out the door as Lisa fed me the details on the run.

Lisa told me about the successful pursuer who had bought some turkey from a nearby grocery store's deli and was able to hand-feed the stray. When the dog got close enough, the woman slipped a lead around the dog's neck. Apparently, our canine fugitive had succumbed to hunger, seduced by the smell of Boar's Head Ovengold Turkey. My wife told me to hurry. The little dog panicked after being caught and the woman seriously considered letting her go, afraid she would hurt herself in the struggle to escape. The dog bucked and thrashed like a wild stallion, lassoed for the first time. Her captor became afraid to touch her.

When I arrived reinforcements had assembled for moral support, but everyone was afraid to touch this little grey dog. We had worked so hard to capture her, but now everyone acted as if she were a ravenous predator. I finally saw her clearly for the first time. Her markings were like a miniature German Shepherd Dog but more silver and grey, perhaps a small Spitz, but with a straight tail instead of curled. The red wound on her hind leg looked ugly, but she was a beautiful little girl.

Though forewarned by everyone, I was determined not to fail this animal a second time. When I looked at her, I saw an exhausted and frightened little dog, not a beast to be feared. I slowed to a more casual pace as I approached and looked for any signs of aggression. Her ears flattened again in the same unhappy position I had seen before. She wanted to run, not bite me. I gently scooped her into my arms and carried her to our van, laying her in the kennel we'd kept set up in the back for the last two weeks. I gripped the rope lead in my hand, in case she managed to wriggle free.

Now, I wanted to calm and comfort the frightened little dog as much as possible. Speaking words in a soft voice seemed the right thing. In the twenty-minute drive to the vet's office, I listened to her whine about her captivity. Preventing a rough ride, I took it slow, using my most soothing voice to comfort her, but it didn't seem to help. A memory. Suzanne sang to this dog on that cold rainy day, and it soothed the savage beast, as the expression goes. Desperate times call for desperate measures. Although I can't carry a tune in a bucket, I sang every song I could remember during those twenty minutes to the vet. Lullabies, hymns, popular tunes, any song I knew words to and made up new lyrics.

Our granddaughter Ava Grace loves to hear me sing, "You Are My Sunshine." I knew a verse or two, so I tried it out on the little grey dog. For some reason she quieted, so I crooned the verses over and over on the last leg of our journey.

When I reached the vet and opened the kennel door, I was pleased the dog didn't try to make a mad dash for freedom. She seemed much calmer than she had been at the bank. I carried her in my arms into an examination room.

The veterinarian examined her and decided she was a Norwegian Elkhound mix. He needed to sedate her to examine her leg, so he suggested he keep her overnight.

The next morning the vet technician brought the grey dog back to me. She looked at me warily, as if she couldn't quite remember me. I spoke to her in the same voice I used to soothe and comfort her the day before. Her whole body quivered with joy — and not just her tail.

I admit it. I fell in love. How do I break the news to my wife? By this time, she wasn't threatened by four-legged competition. But we had promised to help each other keep our resolve strong, to remember not to fall too much in love because, "there is always a next one needing our help." Would I ever be able to say goodbye to this dog?

The vet determined her injury healed enough on its own, so he recommended an antibiotic ointment to help it heal fully. She was ready for the next step, inoculations prior to adoption. That meant she needed to be quarantined for at least ten days to prevent either catching or spreading disease at the shelter. Of course, no other quarantine option came to mind, except my house. I was perfectly happy to add her to the pack, even if it was only temporary. The dog appeared reluctant to bond with anyone but my wife and me.

Once she entered the Humane Society adoption program, the little grey hound needed a means of identification for tracking purposes. She became D5017, the D for dog, and the 5016 dogs that preceded her in the program. Lisa and I agreed we would foster D5017 until she was adopted or she went to the shelter. Of course, I had other ideas in mind for the length of her stay.

Because we have several large dogs as both permanent and foster residents of our home, we segregated our new addition from the pack and planned to introduce them gradually. To get her more accustomed to human contact, I slept with her on the floor of the guest bedroom the first few nights. That strange behavior merited the arching of Lisa's eyebrows. Gradually we mixed her in with the pack, first with the established permanent pack, followed by the less stable members, our foster dogs. After D5017 met everyone, we all went for a walk together.

Calling our first effort a walk is a stretch of the imagination, especially because I carried the new dog most of the way. I put her on the ground to encourage her do her business, but she was so nervous, she chose not to. A whole day passed, and her biological dam burst. It had gotten to the point that I was ready to call the vet, fearing a bowel obstruction or some other serious medical issue.

We named D5017 Gracie, after our granddaughter Ava Grace. They both liked to hear me sing, "You Are My Sunshine." I had worried that Gracie might act inappropriately around the pack. She was so small; I feared she could get hurt. But Gracie proved much more comfortable in the company of other dogs than the company of people.

Briefly we kept Gracie separated from the pack by a wooden child security gate, but she chewed it into splinters in short order. The floor looked littered with a thousand toothpicks.

Lisa has said that we only keep the dogs that are so broken they don't fit anywhere else. I have a slightly different perspective. I think some dogs like Gracie are a bit smarter than others. Unlike our other permanent pack members, Gracie didn't display any pseudo-behavioral problems that only appeared in other homes and disappeared in ours. We knew she wasn't normal from the first day we had her. So, I convinced myself she belonged in our home.

Shortly after we started fostering her, a woman with an autistic daughter called to find out more about her. We shared Gracie's history and her timid temperament. The lady warmed to Gracie's story and thought that perhaps a quiet dog would be a good match for her daughter. If we had to let Gracie go, it could only be for a greater good of helping a child. We got as far as checking our calendars to arrange a meeting, then the mother asked to have overnight to think about it, to be sure she was doing the right thing. Whether she somehow sensed our deep bond with Gracie already, or found a dog she thought was a better match, we never heard from her again.

We formally adopted Gracie from the Humane Society a week later.

We knew Gracie needed us and we needed her. We were not sure at first Gracie felt the same way about her new family. The acid test came. At a nearby park, when I bent to tie my shoe, somehow Gracie pulled her leash out from my grasp. Lisa gave chase, but like a child playing tag, it seemed like fun to Gracie. The harder Lisa chased, the wider the gap grew between them. Gracie ran only so Lisa would chase her. Of course, my wife had no hope of catching her. Eventually she realized this and stopped trying. She positioned herself between Gracie and the park exit, which led out to a dangerous highway. Lisa looked like a hapless linebacker, struggling to fill a huge gap in the line. Gracie played the elite running back, about to shake off her last potential tackler before gaining an unobstructed open field.

I gave up tying my shoelace. I knew I couldn't catch Gracie, with or without my laces tied. More than thirty yards separated us, and she was fast. If I chased her, she would just run in the opposite direction.

I remained kneeled and used my special voice to call her. It was a huge gamble. The stakes were high. Gracie was seconds away from a clean escape. No telling where she would roam. We were far from her old stomping grounds. I could see her waver between the lure of the great unknown and the siren call of my special voice. She made her decision. Gracie ran toward me at breakneck speed. As she drew near, she gave no indication she planned to stop once she reached me. It felt like this might be one last drive-by taunt before she left us for good.

Responsible for losing her once, I wasn't willing to risk it. This could be my only chance. I rationalized, told myself, from my kneeling position, it wouldn't hurt much when I dove face-first toward the asphalt as I grabbed for the leash when Gracie passed by.

I lied. As I grasped the leash, it hurt far more than I expected, but not as much as letting her get away.

Gracie has been with us for several years. I trust her not to run away. Sometimes she looks wild-eyed, as if she doesn't recognize me. To be on the safe side, over the years we have fattened her up just enough to make sure she's a little easier to catch, in case she does try to run off again.

In fact, Lisa has a new nickname for Gracie. She calls her "my little butter bean." Just for the record, her whole body still shakes with joy when I sing "You Are My Sunshine." And she's still a sucker for Boar's Head Ovengold Turkey.

CHAPTER 7
THE DOG WHO LIVED
UNDER GRANDMA'S BED

Following our own creed, "if we keep this one, we can't help the next one," is sometimes harder than others. It took a significant amount of discipline to let go of most of the hundred-plus dogs and cats that passed through our revolving door when the perfect "forever" home came along. It is especially tough after winning a hard-fought breakthrough with a sensitive, damaged creature. I believe there is a home for every dog, and finding that perfect match for even the hardest to place canine is its own reward. Still, it can be hard to let go — hard to trust that the new home will understand and care for the special one as well as we could. This is a story about one such dog that will always live in our hearts.

Pancho may have been the toughest foster challenge we have faced to date. He was well worth the effort.

After my wife and I fostered a dozen or more dogs for our local Humane Society, I thought we had run the gamut of dealing with difficult dog behavior. We learned how to house train puppies and older dogs that lived in the yard for years with equal success. We fostered fear-aggressive and dominance-aggressive dogs alike. We cared for laid-back dogs and hyperactive ones, puppies and older dogs whose owner either died or got too sick to keep them.

I was wrong to think I had seen it all. I found this out when Lisa brought Pancho home.

I stifled a laugh, seeing Pancho for the first time. He looked as if someone painted a basset hound the colors of Rin Tin Tin. The next-door neighbor's German Shepherd Dog mated with his basset hound mother; the genetic combination gave Pancho an abnormally large head upon a  basset hound body, colored with the classic black-and-tan coat of his shepherd father. He had the unfortunate look of a terrified comic strip character.

But I saw a dog suffering.

Lisa shared with me that Pancho came in with his siblings. "When he first arrived at the shelter, a puppy with his siblings, Pancho behaved like any other puppy. As people adopted his brothers, his personality grew withdrawn. I'm certain that no one mistreated him while he was at the shelter. The puppies were so young — he probably couldn't have been abused beforehand, either. I think he is just very sensitive. It's the chaos of the shelter that upsets him so much. The longer he is there, the worse he regresses"

Some dogs are unable to adapt or cope in a shelter environment. Lisa recognized that with Pancho, so she brought him home.

I learned techniques to handle dogs that demonstrate aggression problems. Fear aggression isn't much different from withdrawal, which is like passive fear. I thought this would be easy to turn around. I had no idea the most difficult dog to help would be one afraid of his own shadow.

When Pancho first arrived at our house, he resisted leaving his crate. I opened the kennel door and went outside the house, leaving the exterior door open. It took some time, but he ventured out. But the dog skittered as far from me as possible, maintaining sight of his safe haven. He did his business and shot back into his kennel.

I used every technique I could recall to break through Pancho's defenses, but the dog rebuffed my every effort and distanced himself from accepting my love. With most dogs, sitting outside their kennel and ignoring them for a while would have been enough to rouse their curiosity.

Not Pancho.

With a little patience and a good book to pass the time, a new dog would overcome fear and come close, sniffing around, and just by sheer curiosity. Pancho stayed glued to the opposite side of the kennel, as far away from human contact as possible.

The phrase misery loves company rang in my ears, sort of an inspiration. I felt sorry for Pancho. I began to dwell on anything that would make me miserable, driving out any thoughts of happiness, and this led to a connection with the miserable dog. Three days passed. Pancho found some bravado and ventured near the door of his kennel as I sat in the same room with a show of sadness. Bribery... I wondered if he liked peanut butter like my other dogs. I gave them medicine smeared with a gob of peanut butter and they didn't even know I fooled them.

I held a spoon over my shoulder through the bars of the kennel, my back turned toward him. Pancho took a taste, very reluctantly, but then cleaned the spoon. Thereafter I gave him his bribe off my fingers, associating my scent with good things like food. I didn't want to push him into retreat, so I was content that he ate peanut butter from my fingers, inserted between the bars of the kennel, for another two days. On the third day, I opened the kennel door and dealt with Pancho, no protective barrier between us. I certainly didn't want to drag him out of the kennel, but I couldn't let him cower in there much longer.

The bond between us came with persistence, but it grew. Pancho calmed and extended me his tentative trust.

Dogs are by nature pack animals. They recognize the difference between a human being and another dog. Dogs know they are dogs, but most want to be treated like people. Pancho proved to be an exception — he didn't want to act like a human being or be with people. He had little use for most humans, but Pancho really loved other dogs. His rehabilitation accelerated after we integrated him with the rest of our dog pack. I don't remember him ever meeting another dog he didn't like.

Pancho finally decided to tolerate me, and he loved my wife, but he barked at our son every time he saw him. He was an equal opportunist when it came to showing fear of tall people, short people, grandmothers, and babies. He didn't discriminate based on race, creed, gender, color, religion, or national origin. He shied from just about every human being he saw.

Because our granddaughter Ava Grace had difficulty remembering the names of all the dogs that came and left our home, she called Pancho the dog that lives under Grandma's bed.

As soon as Pancho laid eyes on Ava, especially younger brother Ashton, he ran under our bed and remained there for the rest of their visit. Our grandchildren lived several hundred miles away, so they usually stayed with us for the whole weekend, and Pancho stayed under the bed for the whole weekend.

Meanwhile, more dogs came to us and were adopted into forever homes. Pancho got along with everybody canine. I will always remember with fondness how he chased the beagle Freckles all over our house, and how they both curled together into the smallest ball possible and slept on our bed. The memory of the basset hound Rufus always brings a smile, rollicking with Pancho and flattening a bed of liriope. My favorite memory remains Pancho lying on his back on top of my bed, writhing in pleasure, while I rubbed his belly, because he let me.

Pancho's affections seemed limited to the two of us. As foster dogs came and went, we realized that Pancho would stay a permanent member of our family. Our son Matt heard his baying objections every single day as he braved the trip through the family room from his bedroom; Pancho never warmed up to him.

Saying that the dog feared Matt would be an understatement; the poor thing was so petrified of him that he frequently lost control of his bladder or bowels upon sight. The dog lived just a few steps from abject terror all day long. Of course, we couldn't ask our teenage son to move out, and Pancho had nowhere else to go but back to the shelter. Thank goodness for easy-to-clean wood floors.

After almost a year without an inquiry, a young woman sent Lisa an email, asking about Pancho's availability. "I grew up with basset hound mixed breeds. Your description of his special needs in the Petfinder advertisement I saw on the internet appealed to me. There is something special in his eyes."

Reviewing her adoption application, we hoped that she and Pancho would be a match. If we made a mistake in placing Pancho, it could set him back emotionally, perhaps even permanently. Lisa asked me to go along with her and help her make the decision.

He lived with us for so long that we both wanted to be sure he would be happy in his new home. We arrived at her apartment with mixed feelings, hoping Pancho might finally find his place in this world, but also determined not to let him go into just any home. He'd come a long way, but even now would act threatened by strangers.

A young soft-spoken woman with a kind manner greeted us. My wife and I both liked her instantly. We were amazed to see Pancho relax in her presence as he met her. He normally contact with new people. With the front door safely closed behind us, I loosened my grip on his leash. Instead of furtively darting behind us as we expected, the dog set out and explored her apartment.

I slipped the young woman a bag of his favorite treats, convinced she'd need them as bribes. Pancho ventured near enough to sniff her. She sealed the deal for his affection, rewarding every brave approach with a treat. His cautious, tentative sniffs grew more frequent. Soon Pancho was easily taking what she offered. I felt a pang of jealousy to see how easily he took food from her when it had been so difficult for me.

The last thing Lisa wanted to happen was for Pancho to accept his new home and regress to behavior his new owner couldn't accept. We spent time and disclosed his history in detail, not the least of which, his reaction to young teenage boys.

The young woman smiled brightly, "No worries Pancho. I teach high school. I'm not crazy about teenage boys, either."

We shared a laugh, an instant common denominator for bonding. Pancho had finally found a home where he would never again have to live under the bed.

CHAPTER 8
RUNAWAY RUSTY

Usually, we humans decide to adopt a dog. But sometimes, it works the other way around.

Rusty had experienced a rough life before he came to our house for rescue and rehabilitation. After spending several weeks camped at my wife's feet, he picked up on what life was like for the rest of our pack. When it came time for his adoption, Rusty had obviously developed his own ideas about where his perfect forever home might be..

"Rusty was returned again," Lisa said.

"What did he do this time?" I asked, not terribly surprised.

"The woman who adopted him complained that he kept running away," Lisa said. "She said every time she walked out the front door, he'd make a run for it. She's tired of chasing him all over her neighborhood."

"Rusty?" I asked incredulously. That didn't sound like him at all. "When will you bring him back here?"

"When I go to the shelter on Thursday." And so it was settled.

It wasn't Rusty's first time through our revolving door. The older but beautiful black-and-tan collie had fostered with us more than once since his original owner surrendered him back the shelter.

The woman who had adopted Rusty from the shelter as a puppy returned him after six years with her, claiming he had grown too large for her house and that he was digging up her backyard. As the shelter manager deftly pulled the rest of the story from her, she admitted that once Rusty grew beyond the adorable puppy size, she'd bought a smaller dog and banished Rusty to the backyard for the next five years. All that time, Rusty had watched through the sliding glass doors as the little dog stayed warm and dry, while he was forced to brave the elements.

When the woman brought Rusty back to the shelter after years spent in her yard, his coat was a filthy, matted mess. He was also infected with heartworms. Heartworms are a particularly dangerous condition for collies because of their tendency to have adverse reactions to ivermectin, the drug commonly used for both prevention and treatment. Back in the Humane Society's care, Rusty was cleaned up, groomed, and then began the long course heartworm treatment recommended for collie breeds.

Rusty couldn't be allowed any strenuous exercise because of the controlled poisons used to kill the heartworms, so the bustling excitement of the shelter was not an ideal place for him to recuperate. Lisa brought him to the comparative quiet of our house, where he spent six weeks camped beneath her desk during the day, getting pampered and slipped extra little tidbits of food.

The handsome dog appeared perfectly content just lying around the house, most of the time at Lisa's feet, only needing one or two visits outside per day to pee. The most

energy he expended came at dinner or snack time. Rusty had a voracious appetite, one that bordered on food aggression. I soon learned it was best to feed him just outside the back door so he didn't squabble with the rest of our pack while they ate.

His history of neglect explained his craving for human attention, as well as his extreme fear of thunderstorms. Life at our house must have seemed like heaven, compared to the neglect he left behind. Once he fully recovered and we posted him for adoption on Petfinder.com, the beautiful and highly adoptable Rusty drew plenty of interest from potential adopters.

In fact, he was adopted three times in rapid succession. We were all surprised that each time, the mellow collie was returned for a different offense. One woman said Rusty threatened her cat, chasing it under the bed. Strangely enough, we also had fostered a cat with kittens at our house, and Rusty didn't bother them. In fact, no matter what the complaint when Rusty was returned to the shelter, it was invariably behavior we never saw from the dog.

After he'd been returned for the third time, the shelter manager announced that adoption fees had been collected for Rusty three times, and in each case the adopter refused the refund. The bottom line was that Rusty had paid for himself with his antics, so if Lisa wanted to keep him, she

71

could. We talked it over and agreed our revolving door would swing open once again for Rusty.

"You might as well bring him back and get used to the idea he's your dog," I laughed. I knew Lisa had developed a soft spot for the collie she saw transformed with simple, basic care. "It's what he's wanted all along. Don't you see? Rusty recognized a good deal when he saw it. He decided he wants to live here. That's why he acts up when he goes to a different house. This time, he barely lasted the weekend there. We're the softhearted suckers who cook twice the meat on the grill. One piece is for us and one is for the dogs. And that boy likes to eat too much to leave here without pulling out all the stops."

"You think he's misbehaving on purpose?" Lisa frowned, considering the possibility. "I don't know, but it does sort of seem that way. You might be right."

"You know I'm right, and I'll prove it when you bring him back to the house."

On Thursday, Lisa brought Rusty home as planned. I put our other dogs in the back yard and met them in the foyer, as soon as they walked in the house. "How're ya doing, Rusty?" I said.

He stood there wagging his tail, pleased to receive the attention.

I walked past Lisa and opened the front door. "He kept running away, every time the front door opened, huh?"

Lisa nodded, "That's what the lady said."

"Okay, Rusty, this is your big chance. Go ahead and make your break for it! I won't try to stop you, if you don't want to be here. The door is wide open. Go on, boy! Run for it!"

Rusty looked at me as if I'd lost my mind. His response was to lie down. The matter was settled. With his unmistakable answer, we added Rusty the wayward collie to our pack, the first dog to adopt us instead of the other way around.

"See!" I crowed triumphantly. "I told you, that dog's not going anywhere. This is where he wants to be."

"It's your fault," Lisa said. "You're the one who feeds them."

CHAPTER 9
CHESTER

The biggest toll on the heart doesn't come from having to say goodbye to the dogs and cats we foster, it comes from coping with constant and often bitter disappointment in our fellow humans. Just when I think I have seen the depths of callous indifference people can exhibit toward the animals whose very lives depend on our care, another dog's situation shocks me anew. My cynical shell thickens and I doubt whether we are making any real difference. The very idea that a human being could strike a sweet, lovable beagle in the head with a hammer is a difficult one to accept. But helping the helpless animal is what we do — and the injured beagle fully recovered, going on to a caring forever home. Yet the law of averages says they do not all end happily.

We learned there is a term for this sort of burn out, called compassion fatigue. It is similar to the weary disillusioned apathy that often plagues hospital emergency room doctors and nurses, first responders and soldiers in battle. Working within the Humane Society, we are better equipped to help each other recognize and cope with compassion fatigue. If you are on the front lines of animal rescue and battling these feelings, I encourage you to read about the symptoms of compassion fatigue and coping strategies before you reach the point of burn out. It's better to scale back your efforts and keep helping any way that you can than allow yourself to reach the point where you've got nothing left to give.

The psyches of companion animals are usually more resilient than our own. Dogs don't hold a grudge and will forgive almost any offense in return for being a part of your pack. Not every foster tale is a happy one. Animals that have been tortured or abused are the worst cases.

Chester's tale got off to a rocky start, but at least his story had a happy ending.

My wife knows that it is better to beg forgiveness than to ask permission, so she called to inform me that she was bringing home another dog from the Humane Society shelter after she was already en route. It was a familiar story repeated on a Sunday afternoon, one that happened quite frequently since our son started working part time at the adoption center. With all other alternatives closed, some of the most desperate cases crossed through the shelter's doorway on Sundays.

I began a feeble protest, but Lisa guilted me into submission. "He's just a little guy, a scruffy wire haired terrier mix of some sort. I'm taking him to the vet for evaluation. I am so afraid they are going to recommend euthanizing him to save him more pain. The poor thing can't walk. He must have been hit by a car; the little fellow was dragging his hind legs behind him when a visitor passing through on vacation found him. Some rotten little kids in a subdivision were taunting the poor thing, throwing stones at him and acting like they were about to kick him.

After the man rescued the dog, he had no idea what to do. He looked up the Humane Society in the phone book, got our address, and brought us the dog. We couldn't turn him away, but you know we don't have any empty kennels. Besides, you can't leave a dog that's in this bad a shape in a kennel and let him suffer overnight. Matt and I are taking him to the emergency vet before we come home. This poor little guy probably won't ever make it home with us, anyway. Like I already said, the vet will probably recommend we put him down," her voice cracked with emotion.

My feeble attempts to protest thoroughly crushed by guilt, I asked, "So, what do you want me to go pick up for supper?"

The following morning the vet called Lisa. The excitement in her voice was palpable. "You won't believe it," she exclaimed. He's standing on his own!"

"Wow!" Lisa said, "How did that happen? He must be one tough little guy."

"I'd have to agree with you. I didn't do anything but give him some pain medication and a little TLC. He's done the hard work on his own."

Lisa said, "Does he need surgery? What else can we do for him?"

"Take him home," the vet replied. "Be careful letting him around the big dogs at your house. He could be a little short-tempered because his legs hurt, and if he snaps at one of your German Shepherds, he could become a quick hors d'oeuvre."

Lisa promised she would watch out for him when she reached home.

I got my first opportunity to meet the tough little guy when Lisa arrived home with him. With a wiry medium length coat colored in blond and black streaks, his body was longer than it was tall because of his short stubby legs. The tips of his ears curled forward and his bright eyes peered out over a wild, thick moustache. He wriggled to get out of her arms, anxious to mingle with our pack of dogs.

"I'm not supposed to let him mix with the bigger dogs in case he gets hurt" she managed to say as she struggled to keep him in her arms. She tried her best to keep him nestled next to her chest, but the little bundle of energy strained continuously to escape.

Following the vet's instructions, Lisa asked me to erect the crate we kept for such occasions while she held the dog aloft, protecting him from the curiosity of the pack. For ten long days, he chafed at his confinement as we kept him segregated from the larger dogs. The vet feared an inadvertent bump from one of the much larger pack members could displace his healing pelvis, so we committed to following her adamant instructions to curtail his activity. For the first seven days, pain medication dulled his senses and suppressed his spunky demeanor to some degree, but by the end of his quarantine, the medicine and his patience ran out simultaneously. Mellow when doped up, when the drugs ran out, the feisty little dog quickly accumulated some serious pent-up energy, and an attitude to match.

Finally, the day came we could allow our hospital patient to mingle with the pack. Lisa carried him into the kitchen. The pack milled around her feet, sniffing at the little terrier squirming in her arms with all his might, struggling to get down and smell the big dogs. Finally, I said, "Don't worry about it. With both of us standing right here watching all of them, we'll be able to snatch him off the ground in an instant, at the first sign of trouble."

Lisa reluctantly agreed and gently set the dog on the floor. The terrier immediately introduced himself to the other dogs and began trailing in the footsteps of the large German Shepherds, just wanting to be accepted as part of the pack.

"He sure is a tough little guy," I said. "You said the vet diagnosed him with a fractured pelvis?"

"Yes, she was amazed he could stand on his own and walk without assistance. He's not supposed to be able to do it," Lisa said. "She said it isn't a break that can be set. It needs time to heal on its own."

His right hind leg didn't bend like the left as he limped and hopped around the kitchen island behind the pack. "We still haven't given him a name. Have you thought of one?" I asked Lisa.

"Honey, deciding on a name hasn't been a foremost concern in my mind. I worried about whether or not we could keep him safe here with all these larger dogs. But apparently, he thinks he is as big as they are. He's a feisty little one, isn't he?"

"He sure is. A name just popped into my head. Do you remember the character Dennis Weaver played on Gunsmoke before he left to become McCloud?

Lisa nodded in agreement, but I think she was humoring me.

Guessing she had no clue but was not eager to set me off on a tangent, I continued my line of thought, "Dennis Weaver's character on the show limped around all the time. They called him Chester. Why don't we name this little guy 'Chester' since he's got a bum leg, too?"

Lisa shrugged and said, "Works for me. We haven't fostered a 'Chester' before. It's an easy name to remember, unique."

The gutsy little dog now had a name.

He proved to be a truly amazing dog. We had only just begun to learn about his tenacious personality and just how tough he was.

Chester immediately took to running with the pack, except he limped and hobbled after the bigger dogs as fast as he could. Like a smaller child emulating his big brother, the little terrier had to do everything the big dogs did. This included marking territory on the biggest oak tree closest to the deck behind our house.

Ox sauntered over to the tree and hiked his leg. When he finished doing his business, the terrier hopped over and tried to follow suit. But Chester faced two major problems. First, mere moments earlier he had squatted and relieved himself. Second, his fractured hip made it extremely painful to hike his leg.

The quick-witted little dog improvised a simple but brilliant solution. He performed a "handstand" on his front paws and let his hind legs rest lightly against the tree trunk. It looked like he was gritting his teeth until he managed to squeeze out a couple more drops of urine where Ox marked his territory and softly dropped to the ground, satisfied he had established himself as boss of the back yard. Later I noticed that an endearing under-bite meant his teeth looked perpetually gritted in determination.

Practically overnight, he developed enough strength to perform his handstand trick without supporting himself on the tree. Within a few days, his hindquarters were strong enough that he could bear enough weight to hike his leg. He continued to heal and showed no lingering signs of pain, no sensitivity to touch. He was as likely to lie on his right side as his left. However, his right hind leg never again bent normally, leaving him with a permanent limp in his gait.

The scruffy terrier didn't have a shy bone in his body. He would bark to inform his humans that it was time for treats, bark at passing traffic, bark to go outside, and bark to be picked up and held. He tried to challenge the bigger dogs for their treats, convincing me the dog had a death wish. From day one, Chester believed he ruled the roost. Convinced he owned the place, he acted as if we must have been hard pressed to manage without his alert instructions.

Once we knew he was healthy and adoptable, we prepared to find Chester his perfect home. He was not one destined to remain forever on our "island of misfits." He was simply too cute and highly adoptable, once his legs healed well enough. We loved the little terrier and cared for him through the time he needed us the most. Chester gave us his over-sized love in return.

A dog with that much personality, an adorably photogenic face, and an inspirational story like his always attracts a lot of attention from well-qualified potential adopters. Chester proved no exception. His adoption posting included his back-story. It drew a tremendous response, and Chester found his forever home with a retired couple who love to travel around the country in their R.V.

He goes wherever they do, hopping around the campsites to guard the perimeter and mark his territory in his trademark handstands, but now he does it just to show off. Occasionally his human companions will send a new postcard to the Humane Society to remind us how well he is loved.

And, of course, Chester rules his new roost, no matter from where the postcard originates.

CHAPTER 10
SIMON/SIMONE

Prioritizing which dogs and cats our small Humane Society took into our adoption program was always more art than science. When every foster home is full to the brim, every kennel at the shelter is occupied, and the cat rooms are at capacity, how do you make room for one more? As a matter of philosophy, our Humane Society operated a no-kill program. That meant once an animal came into our care, it was safe. We would not euthanize for space or treatable conditions. The down side to that meant when our program was full, we had to maintain a waiting list for people wanting to surrender animals. In contrast, the animal shelter operated by the county was open-admission. That meant they accepted any animal any time, as long as the person surrendering the animal could provide proof of county residence. But when their shelter was full, they euthanized for space.

Given the two choices, people often found creative ways to sneak animals into our care — also known as abandonment, in spite of county ordinances prohibiting it.

In spite of perimeter fencing, it was not uncommon to find a dog or cat waiting on the doorstep of our adoption center upon opening in the morning. Knowing we would not take the animal to the county shelter, the prior caregiver managed to skip to the front of the line by abandoning the animal rather than be bothered with the waiting list. When that happened, we had to pull yet another small miracle out of the air and create a temporary spot for our new, unexpected charge.

It should not be much of a surprise by now to learn that we typically fostered dogs, considering the number of canine misfits who became permanent residents in our home and the foster stories you've read to this point. However, occasionally, a special cat comes along that needs a temporary home. Meet Simon. Or, should I say, Simone.

One night our son Matt found an abandoned cat outside the Humane Society as he closed for the night. The cat had been secured inside a plastic-shell pet carrier left next to the front door. Matt called the cat Simon; the name was neatly printed in block letters on a piece of tape that adorned the plastic roof above the carrier's wire mesh door. Because the cat had been abandoned with no veterinary records, Matt had to bring Simon home. He knew that unvaccinated strays posed a risk to cats already housed at the shelter. The two rounds of shots required a ten-day quarantine period as part of the protocol.

By this time in our fostering years, we had moved into a smaller split — level home, downsizing with the economic downturn like so many others we knew. The home still offered a nice, large back yard and our fostering continued. Unfortunately, we were on the main thoroughfare through the large neighborhood, giving our dogs plenty to bark at throughout the day. Still living at home to save money while he attended college in Atlanta, Matt knew the potential impact of bringing a cat into our smaller home, but he saw no alternative. He was the last one to leave and lock up. He could either leave the poor cat confined in the carrier in the lobby overnight, or bring Simon home until more suitable arrangements could be found.

He phoned Lisa to explain the situation and offer advance warning. We braced ourselves, watching for his headlights in the driveway.

When Matt came inside with this cat crouching in his carrier, their arrival caused a great deal of interest in our house. He held the small carrier high on his shoulders and rushed upstairs away from the rest of the household.

We are a dog-friendly family; the current pack of permanent and foster dogs in unison vociferously protested the addition of a feline. Even worse than the barking, the dogs milled at the bottom of the stairs, silently waiting for the moment the cat made his fatal mistake, following curiosity to its dangerous conclusion.

None of us dared to test pack motives; it seemed we made a prudent decision, separating the cat and the dogs, until Simon was placed in a more suitable sanctuary. I installed two baby gates on our stairwell, which blocked off the bedrooms from the living area. A gate placed at the bottom prevented the dogs from coming upstairs, and the second gate at the top served as an additional defensive barrier. Simon had the run of the upstairs, and the dogs ruled the downstairs. Actually, because of my allergies and because I had no reason to bond with the cat, Simon stayed in the guest bedroom.

Released from his carrier, I noticed that Simon appeared an attractive long-haired cat with a distinctive tabby mask and tail. His beautiful long white fur made it impossible for me to spot any surgical scars that would confirm that he had been neutered. I made a surgical appointment with the vet for a complete exam.

Meanwhile, finding another foster opening for Simon proved futile. In spite of the dogs, ours was the only roof available for his head, being such an unanticipated arrival into the Humane Society program.

A couple of days later, Simon went under the knife. A very perplexed vet called us a few hours later, letting me know Simon was a female cat. The neuter procedure changed to a spay surgery, mid-operation. The vet then discovered Simon, now named Simone by necessity, had already undergone a full hysterectomy.

The indignity of the belly shave, the effects of the anesthesia, and the needless surgery made Simone one grumpy cat. I took some pity on her and allowed her out to visit the other upstairs bedrooms. She seemed fond of Matt's room, perhaps, because she recognized him as her rescuer, and began to hang out there. Matt learned more about her personality, telling us every one of his discoveries. One day he said, "Simone thinks she's a dog!"

I asked him what he meant.

"When the rest of the dogs barked at the garbage truck, Simone joined in, growling just like she was one of them!"

I laughed along, not sure if Matt was serious, and chalked it up as the vivid imagination of a bored college student. Our son worked two days this month filling in at the shelter, because in the slow summer economy, he couldn't find a steadier job. One of those work days, he brought this cat home.

But as far as cats go, he couldn't have picked a better one. After a while, I changed my perception. Simone didn't think she was one of the dogs. She appointed herself their queen. She would perch at the top of the stairs, impervious to the irritation and whining she roused in her subjects below, and lorded over them with calm disdain.

Occasionally Simone ventured down the stairs and gave face to face affront to the pack.

I grew to see that Simone liked to follow people around, just hang out with the human beings, which seemed more like dog behavior than cat. Simone's fur didn't aggravate my allergies like other cats. I knew how attached Matt had become to the cat; we entertained thoughts we might adopt her. I had to consider that one of the big dogs could hurt this gentle soul, should she circumvent the barriers, so I had

to abandon ownership for Matt and post her adoption information on the shelter's website. We could enjoy her as a foster in our home, but her best option for a forever home did not include life among a pack of large dogs.

Simone had a personality unlike any other cat I had ever known. Her demeanor was very unique. Her manner was friendly, without a hostile bone in her body, and she never demanded attention, but she always stood aloof. I could read her emotions like a book. When I tried to pick her up, though I gripped her at both side securely, she tried to escape and gave a look I could see meant she didn't want to be held. When I lifted her, she'd squirm a little and then go limp as a rag doll. I knew that once her efforts, halfhearted it seemed, proved futile, she made the most of it, started purring, and settled in.

Lisa and I cataloged her eccentric behavior and compared notes. She researched the internet and identified these unusual characteristics as associated with a type called the rag doll cat. Simone appeared to be a textbook example of a rag doll. Her only characteristic that didn't match the prototypical description of the breed were her amber eyes; they would typically appear blue.

Within a month, an older couple submitted an application and seemed to be a perfect match for Simone. The couple decided to open their home to a new cat after grieving for their deceased pet. These folks proved they were the right choice and their home would be great for Simone. But we now faced a challenge. How could we let someone else adopt this wonderful cat with whom the entire family — except the dogs — fell in love?

We reminded ourselves how Simone came to us in the first place. If we held on to her, that eliminated one more possible miracle out of thin air when the next cat was abandoned on a doorstep. And so, we said goodbye. Fostering has bittersweet rewards.

CHAPTER 11
MEMPHIS VERSUS THE MIGHTY OX

Dogs are truly resilient creatures, but that is not to say their life experiences can't leave emotional scars. The vast majority of the dogs we fostered thrived under consistent care, pack order and affection. But a few sensitive souls needed extra help. I continue to be amazed how intuitively our own dogs tuned into the needs of these special ones. Memphis was badly broken when he came to our house. He was rudely ripped out of the only home he had ever known as the only dog there, and thrust into the cacophony of the Humane Society dog run building. But never underestimate the healing power of a stable pack. Dogs can be great at fostering other dogs. Our pack helped heal Memphis, and set him on his way to becoming a more normal dog.

This was one matchup of David versus Goliath where David never stood a chance, and was very lucky this particular Goliath has a heart of gold.

Compassion overwhelmed my wife Lisa when she saw Memphis and his pathetic mental state. She only needed a way to make me aware of his plight. A medium-sized Australian shepherd mix, afraid of his own shadow, someone had to place him into a forever home before the effects of shelter life did permanent damage.

Originally adopted from the Humane Society as a puppy, the dog lived a happy life with his family for more than six years. When their youngest child left for college, the parents decided they no longer had time to spend with Memphis. They gave him back to the Humane Society, knowing our policy of always taking our animals back. Returns go to the top of the priority list, sending us scurrying for miracles just like abandonments on the doorstep.

Even after gentle counseling by adoption center staff trained to convince people to their honor commitments, the parents were resolute, having somehow convinced themselves that Memphis was lonely now that their children were gone and they could not accommodate him in their own busy schedules. With self-serving logic, these adults were sure Memphis would be better off by being uprooted from the only home he had ever known.

Lisa sensed he needed a stable and loving foster environment and wanted to bring him home. With a hidden agenda that I learned later, she walked me through the dog kennel area, so I would see how miserable and pitiful Memphis looked. While this shelter didn't euthanize animals, which was their policy, this dog had never lived with another dog. But suddenly, he now lived in an enclosed kennel housed in a large building with a cacophony of barking dogs. Memphis huddled in the far recesses of his run, shaking in fright. The dog left with us when we went home.

His first attempt to adapt to a foster home failed miserably. The newcomer quickly grew jealous of the permanent dog in the home and showed minor signs of aggression. The foster caregiver brought Memphis back to the shelter where he again became a nervous wreck. He did not know how to interact with other canines or acclimate to their presence.

We have an established dog pack in our home that Lisa calls the core four Shiloh, a large black and tan German Shepherd that we permanently foster due to his medical issues; Gracie, the queen who rules the roost; Rusty, an older collie-mix, a mama's boy; and the unchallenged leader of the pack, Ox. A giant solid black German Shepherd Dog, he's about 95 pounds of solid muscle. When Memphis temporarily joined our family, he attempted to assert himself as alpha dog, usurping Ox's place at my heel.

That did not bode well for his life expectancy. Most dogs fostered at our home developed social skills to understand their place in a dog pack. They all enjoy the freedom of roaming the yard and exploring our home, released from their former shelter restrictions, but they all know beyond doubt, Lisa and I are pack leaders. Ox was the first dog I rescued and adopted, and he's fiercely devoted to me. He's also twice the size of Memphis.

Memphis had not spent much time in the great outdoors. He went outside to do his business if a human being accompanied him, but he acted afraid outside the house. As soon as he finished his call of  nature, Memphis zipped inside, unlike the rest of our pack.

Lisa compared his personality to TV's Adrian Monk — it's a jungle out there.

Despite these quirks of behavior, Memphis challenged Ox as pack leader. Their first fight began and ended within a few seconds. Memphis attacked Ox without provocation and suffered dire consequences. Ox defended himself without injury, actually restraining himself as he caused Memphis only minor damage, a small bloody cut above his eyes. But this was not the end of his challenge. Memphis never attacked any of the other dogs, only Ox, as if he had a death wish. The bigger dog put his attacker in his proper place, using amazing restraint, and he never settled the fights like I knew he could.

Memphis often lost control and attacked Ox when he got excited, for instance, if company came to the house or Lisa was cooking dinner. He worked himself into a frenzy, racing in circles around the tables and through the kitchen, barking and yelping with reckless abandon. Most of these episodes escalated, and he snapped at Ox, and the smaller dog always fared worse than his intended victim. These skirmishes grew more and more frequent.

One night at dinner Memphis lost control attacked Ox once more. The rest of the pack cleared space for the two dogs to square off. When I restrained Ox by his collar, Lisa yelled, "Let Ox go! He can't defend himself. Memphis is being the aggressor."

I let go and grabbed my handy tennis racquet, an excellent "wedge" tool to separate two dogs without hurting them or suffering dog bite. Ox charged forward and knocked Memphis down. He rolled Memphis onto his back and grabbed the smaller dog's throat in his jaws. With a chomp down of his jaws, Memphis would be dead. I believe that both animals realized this. Things got quiet. Ox removed his mouth but used his giant paw to keep him pinned to the ground. He towered over him and glared into the smaller dog's eyes, as if he dared Memphis to move. Ox had had enough of this nonsense. The fight ended. Decisively and without question, Ox emerged, the victor.

After that confrontation, Memphis mellowed in character and attitude. He accepted his place in our house and the love we offered. The healing process began, leading Memphis into a new life as a happier dog among canine and human alike.

CHAPTER 12
SIBLING RIVALRY

Once we aligned our rescue efforts with an organized Humane Society, our involvement was not incremental, but instantaneous. The number of lives we helped did not increase by a slow trickle, but with the force of a faucet opened to its fullest. I described it as akin to "drinking from the fire hose."

Going from zero to 100 miles per hour is an appropriate analogy. It is what theorists call "learning by immersion." Within a year, we could ascertain not only a primary but also secondary and tertiary breed on any new dog. We could diagnose kennel cough from pneumonia before the vet visit. Distinguishing fear aggression from dangerous-dog rehabilitation became second nature. If this sounds like jumping on a roller coaster mid-flight, that means you are beginning to get the idea.

There are no college degrees to prepare us for the intensity of the front lines of animal rescue. Every life is precious. Resources are limited. Ideals are lofty. The pressure to make the most of every opportunity can be daunting.

Along this journey, we experience, observe, and postulate truisms. Whether any of these postulates will prove true in the long term is less relevant. Our ability to recognize patterns and avoid making repetitive mistakes allows us to deploy scarce resources effectively.

This tale explains why it is seldom wise that siblings from the same litter be adopted by one family.

Some jerk dumped two little black Labrador retriever mixed breed puppies onto the southbound emergency lane on GA 400, a busy expressway connecting the northern suburbs to the city of Atlanta. Cars zoomed by the confused, terrified puppies as they edged precariously closer to the tires, asphalt, and metal beasts that would surely mean their death.

A construction manager driving down from Tennessee to quote for work on a jobsite in midtown Atlanta saw them tumbling and scampering on the side of the highway. He really wanted to keep driving, pretending he hadn't seen them—ignoring their peril like so many other drivers either too busy or too calloused to stop and help. With a deep sigh and while cursing under his breath, he stopped his truck.

After driving more than three hours to get to my interview on time, I'm going to make myself late by messing around with these dogs, the man fumed at himself. No good deed goes unpunished.

The two puppies cowered as the man approached, scared out of their minds. His heart quickly filled with pity for the helpless, doomed creatures. The gruff man scooped up the two puppies and headed for the nearest exit, looking for some safe haven or a kindly soul to take them off his hands. As luck would have it, the next exit was the busiest in our suburban county, leading to the main shopping district of

Market Boulevard. His spirits lifted when he spied a Petsmart sign and a row of canvas pop-up pavilions indicating that a rescue group was there holding pet adoptions.

Maybe I will still make that interview on time after all!

Leaving the pups in the bed of his truck, he approached the nearest volunteer. She smiled brightly with hope that he would be a potential adopter. The expression on her face changed dramatically when he conveyed he didn't want to take but rather leave a couple more homeless dogs. The man explained that he was a stranger in town, just passing through. He was from Tennessee, headed to an appointment in Atlanta. Our suburban county was still many miles away from his destination. He didn't even know where to find the nearest animal control facility.

We had to tell him that we could not accept stray pets there at the adoption event. Regretfully, we gave him directions to the animal control, knowing that solid black puppies were less likely to be adopted and may eventually face euthanasia for lack of space at the county shelter.

Though the man arrived during open hours, the county shelter employees told him they had to refuse the puppies because he could not prove residency in the county. It was strict animal control policy not to accept animals from outside communities.

The man was incredulous. I'm not local to the county. But the puppies are!

The stranger in a strange county faced a dilemma. He had two young puppies that were not his problem. He had business in Atlanta. The local county animal shelter steadfastly refused to take the dogs from him. Discouraged, he drove back to the store where he found us earlier.

During the hour that passed since his initial visit, we were having a banner adoption day and spirits were high. Luck would have it that several pets had been adopted into their forever homes that day, freeing a few of the portable metal crates we used at offsite events. The man explained his predicament to our team of volunteers. The Good Samaritan was so frustrated with animal control he threatened to take the puppies and leave them where he originally found them.

We made a hard decision to break with our own protocol, bend the rules, and take the puppies.

The puppies were confused and frightened by the cacophonous barking and bustling swarm of people grabbing and cooing at them. One got away and crawled under the truck, cowering in fear as many hands grabbed frantically at him. Cars zipped around the parking lot competing for spaces, adding an element of danger and sense of urgency to the capture. If the dog managed to wriggle free on the wrong side of the vehicle, it could end in disaster. Finally, someone got a hand on the puppy and extracted him from underneath the vehicle, and the man was gratefully on his way.

My wife Lisa, the adoption team leader that day, separated one of the empty crates from the other dogs in an attempt to adhere to our quarantine policy. For the safety of all, every animal coming into the Humane Society adoption program with an unknown vaccination history must be isolated from other dogs in the program for at least ten days.

She waved me over to help. As I leaned in to spread out a blanket for the pups, she fretted...

"I'm going to get so much grief about this. I can't take them to our Humane Society shelter. There isn't room for them there. I always lecture new volunteers about not breaching protocol, drilling into their brains all the reasons why we can't accept intakes at an offsite event. Here I am doing exactly that. 'Do as I say, not as I do.'"

I knew where this conversation was headed. If she was going to be the one to break the rules that meant she better be willing to own the problem. Lacking any other ready volunteers from the event that day, the puppies would need to come to our home for the duration of their quarantine. Our pack was current on their vaccines and preventives, so they posed little risk to the puppies, or vice versa.

"Surprise, dear. It looks like we are fostering puppies again," my wife said to me apologetically.

One of the wiggling puppies licked my face with a warm, wet tongue. Any misgivings I had about taking in the puppies melted away.

Whenever a new dog came to our home, it became my responsibility to make sure our existing pack accepted them without issues. If behavioral issues were evident, I would take the lead responsibility on the dog's rehabilitation efforts because I worked from home.

But integrating puppies into the pack was usually easy — at least for our other dogs. We humans got the more challenging duty of teaching the young ones house manners.

Bringing home two puppies recently weaned from their mother was a recipe for trouble. They weren't housetrained. They fought constantly. Little puppy growls, snarls and squeals grew so frequent and annoying that we decided to separate them, setting up a second kennel.

Of course, they also loved each other, frequently curling up together in a two-headed black ball when they settled for naps on their own. And they were undeniably cute. How could anyone not love a puppy?

So the male and female lab puppies settled in as our temporary houseguests. The first step was naming them. The Humane Society assigned them numbers them for unique identification, usually leaving name selection to the foster family. We had a leg-hiker and a squatter. The male was dubbed Jethro and the female Ellie Mae, in honor of the rough-and-tumble country cousins on the old The Beverly Hillbillies television show.

The puppies fought like the characters on the show, and true to form, most often Ellie Mae whipped up on Jethro.

I jokingly suggested, "Wouldn't it be great if the same home adopted both puppies?"

Lisa looked at me as if I'd suddenly lost my mind. "Two puppies from the same litter usually adjust better if they don't go into the same home. These two will always compete like this. It's the law of nature, the sibling rivalry. They may never get into a really vicious fight, but they'll probably bicker like this constantly. Forever." She paused to let me imagine Jethro and Ellie Mae going at it like this for years upon years. I gulped and shook the image from my mind.

"Plus, if one is more submissive than the other, the less assertive puppy may never get a chance to thrive out from under the more dominant one's shadow. Siblings also tend to bond more closely with each other than with their human family." She paused to pry Jethro's teeth carefully off her right earlobe as Ellie Mae tugged at her hair.

"It's hard enough for the average family to bring in one new puppy. It's a rare home that can raise two puppies at the same time, giving each of them the individual attention they need. I know it's tempting to keep puppies together, but siblings adopted together are almost twice as likely to be returned to the shelter as puppies that are adopted separately. I always try to encourage families to adopt one puppy, wait a few months, then come back to adopt a second puppy."

"So let's try to find good — separate — homes for these two little clowns," she chuckled.

The puppies were adorable and got along well with the big dogs. They just fought constantly with each other, like most brothers and sisters do at such a young age. Each sibling truly seemed to bring out the worst in the other.

Between their first and second round of shots, I made it my job to housetrain them. A well-mannered dog is much more adoptable than a dog that needs basic training.

Normally, it's a piece of cake. Training a dog to relieve itself outside is not rocket science. As long as I worked at home for several days in a row and used the dog kennels properly, it should not be a problem. The key to housetraining a dog is to eliminate its opportunities to have an accident inside. Keep the dog crated overnight, and when he or she cannot be kept under constant observation. As soon as the dog comes out of the kennel, take it outside immediately.

Have a code word of encouragement that lets the animal know it is time to do their business. "Hurry up" is my favorite. It is a short phrase of encouragement and a reminder it's time. More importantly, it's something I learned to stop saying to my wife a long time ago, so there's no danger of accidentally saying the magic words in the wrong place, at the wrong time.

Lavish praise upon the animal after successful completion of business and the job of housetraining is basically done.

The trick to this technique is making absolutely sure the dogs "get it." This is done by giving them the opportunity for failure while they are under close observation so you can catch them in the act and give negative reinforcement for the "accident," followed by taking them outside to remind them where they are supposed to go.

"Catching" them after the fact is too late.

I took the puppies outside to do business. Afterward, I let them roam free but I kept an eye on them. When I caught Ellie Mae squatting to do business in the house, I yelled "No!" in a stern voice and took her outside, where I issued the "Hurry up" command. Even if it was too late, it communicated where it was acceptable to do business and where it was not.

It is very important to housetrain a dog properly by eliminating every excuse for the adoptive family to stick him or her outside to become a "yard dog." Most dogs catch on with the first correction or two. Generally, the dog's age, intelligence, comprehension abilities, and whether or not the dog has a stubborn streak will determine whether additional corrections are necessary. Even young puppies like Jethro and Ellie Mae normally get with the program by the second or third correction.

Within a couple of days, Jethro seemed completely housetrained, but Ellie Mae still gave us problems. I never caught her having an accident during the day, but for some reason she seemed unable to go overnight without wetting inside her kennel.

She was old enough to make it through the night — after all Jethro was doing fine. I wondered if she might have urinary tract infection or some problem with her kidneys. Until I got to the bottom of the mystery, Jethro gained freedom to roam the house, but Ellie Mae stayed crated unless I could watch her like a hawk.

Perhaps I should make an appointment with the veterinarian to have her checked out, I thought. Something is wrong that she cannot hold her bladder any longer than she does. I hate keeping her crated so much, but until she stops peeing in her kennel, I am hesitant to let her roam the house freely.

The mystery was solved before I called the vet, saving me the embarrassment of taking a perfectly healthy puppy to the clinic for no reason.

Ellie Mae had no problem.

The next morning and I took the puppies outside before breakfast. I watched as both dogs did their business. So far, so good. I brought both puppies back inside and checked Ellie Mae's bedding. It was completely dry. She made it through the night without having an accident in the kennel. I was so proud of her.

I left her free to roam the house and began loading the dishwasher. In a moment of silence unbroken by the clatter of dishes, I heard that unmistakable sound made by a stream of urine. To my great surprise, I saw Jethro in Ellie Mae's kennel, his leg hiked and aimed at her bedding.

This dog had peed outside less than ten minutes ago. This seemed to be a clear-cut case, a spiteful and deliberate act of pure mischievousness. That dog knew exactly what he was doing. Cause and effect — peeing in the house got a dog into trouble. So Jethro didn't just pee anywhere inside the house. He chose the one spot where he could be certain Ellie Mae would suffer the blame. She spent more time locked in the kennel as punishment, leaving him free roam where she could not terrorize him.

The very thought boggled my mind — he framed her!

What would Uncle Jed say? "I think I need to have a long talk with that boy."

CHAPTER 13
SPITFIRE

When the list of dogs and puppies we counted as prior fosters reached into the dozens, my own confidence in dog rehabilitation grew. I knew how to read a raised or tucked tail, measure eye contact and win trust with peanut butter. My skill in house training, leash training and simple obedience training grew with practice. Handling each new, unknown dog and integrating him successfully into the pack added to my expertise. I would never say it became easy because each new dog is unique and unpredictable, but I did settle into a workable routine.

Cats are quite another story. I doubt I will ever become proficient at cat training, as much as cat "negotiating." Some foster animals leave you with lasting memories.

Spitfire left us with lots of little scars. Literally.

"There's a kitten in foster care that can't go to the shelter," my wife Lisa said. "The foster mom can't keep her anymore, because her landlord complained. Where can she go?"

Whenever there was "no place else for an animal to go," our house became the critter refuge of last resort. I wondered how many animals have had their lives depend upon the availability of our house. Yes, we received joy in saving lives, though I often grumbled about the perpetual revolving door of animals — I secretly enjoyed having them. Most of them.

And then we fostered Spitfire. Before bringing home this diminutive flea-ridden bundle of attitude, Lisa forewarned me, the kitten is disabled. She is missing her right front leg.

We put her in the safety of the guest bedroom and let her out of the carrier. The kitten burst out of her cage in full attack mode, crazed by her incarceration. She bit and scratched us, anything she could to deny our offered affection.

Then there were the fleas. I suggested we bathe her. Lisa's exasperation reflected on her face, conveying in detail what she thought of the idea. My wife applied a dry powered flea treatment on the cat, and, within a few days, the problem was solved.

Next project, naming the cat. I suggested Tripod, a play on her physical condition. Lisa ignored me. After a few days, Lisa again mentioned the cat's lack of a name. She explained that she couldn't post the kitten's adoption profile online without a name. I repeated my suggestion of a name for her, Tripod.

"Sweetheart, how many three-legged dogs or cats have you known in your life?" I read condescension in her voice, the best patience she could come up with.

"Three or four, I guess."

"How many of them were called Tripod?"

I didn't like the rejection, but Lisa has never been a big fan of puns. The kitten went without a name a while longer. I began calling her Fleabag, even though I knew she was cured. Lisa suggested that the kitten's personality should dictate the selection of her name. I worked on that. Handicapped would be a poor choice of words for advertising, but Overcompensating seemed much more appropriate. Vicious worked, too.

The little fur ball proved not to have an affectionate bone in her body, especially when we retired for the night. She hunched and arched her back like a witch's black cat, except she was orange calico. Without much warning, she'd would spring into the air and pounce on an unsuspecting foot moving under the covers — while the person attached to the foot was fast asleep. Because she lacked two front paws with which to trap her prey, the kitten used her needle sharp teeth more frequently than normal cats. Every member of our household soon bore tiny scars to remind them of our little Spitfire. Lisa probably came up with the name first, but in reality, the kitten named herself, Spitfire.

Not completely anti-social, Spitfire liked to play, but it always felt more like she toyed with prey intending to kill and eat it. As soon as she got bored, someone paid the price.

Carrying this cat was no fun. My forearms got covered with superficial bite and scratch marks. I received deeper scratches on my chest and stomach, where she used her hind legs as a springboard, escaping from any affection I wanted to show her.

She gave us a scare one day. I had a toy similar to a pompom, with a long tassel of plastic streamers. Spitfire loved to attack it. We played for a while. I laughed when I saw how winded she'd become; Spitfire panted like a dog. I didn't know that cats aren't supposed to pant like dogs — it's a sign of respiratory distress. She began to convulse as I put her back into her room. I yelled, "Lisa! The kitten is having a seizure!"

Lisa raced upstairs, grabbed the kitten, wrapped her in a towel, and forced her finger into Spitfire's mouth, she said, to keep her from biting her tongue. I ran for the cell phone and punched in the vet's number. By that time Spitfire threw up a piece of a streamer that she'd swallowed. I threw the rest of the toy into the trash. We chose safer objects for play, like the kitten mitten, a glove with long wire fingers, with which we wrestled with Spitfire from a safe distance.

I realized she would soon lose her kitten cuteness and become hard to find her "forever" home. The longer we procrastinated, rehabilitating her bad behavior, the longer it would take to place her. We weren't doing Spitfire any favors, allowing her anti-social behavior to continue. But Spitfire liked to be around people. I suspected, proximity made it easier for her to inflict pain, but affection remained a foreign concept. Lisa expressed concerns when our allergies worsened, a big reason why we don't have cats living in our home for very long. And Lisa feared that Spitfire was not adoptable. I thought up a strategy to communicate affection to the kitten.

I brought Spitfire into our bedroom several times each day, But instead of releasing her to play, I held her until she would permit affection. If she struggled and resisted, I took her back to her bedroom, left her for a few minutes, and tried again. I was determined to train the kitten enough so that she would allow me to pet her.

It only took a few days before Spitfire got the message. If she wanted to be around people, she had to allow human affection in return for the reward of play. She quickly learned to keep her claws retracted and to mouth her humans gently, instead of biting them hard enough to draw blood. Spitfire still bit and scratched us, because that was her way to tell us she wanted back in her room. While I trained her, she trained me.

The day finally came when Lisa took Spitfire to the shelter. She had grown and it was time, however sad to say goodbye. Soon her future parents would find the kitten and take her to her forever home. Our scars have all healed, and we knew she never intended to hurt anyone. Nevertheless, our hearts took on some pain...when we parted with our little Spitfire.

CHAPTER 14
BESSIE THE BASSET HOUND

Not every foster dog came to us through the usual Humane Society pleas for help. I admit, I carried a small bag of treats and a couple of slip leads in my car and fell into the habit of stopping when I spied a stray dog. I realized I was unconsciously following in my father's footsteps. Decades ago, before the animal rescue movement gained momentum in the South, my dad was a traveling salesman. He always kept a bag of dog food in the trunk of his car. No strays went hungry if he passed them along his travels. I guess it was inevitable that some of that same sense of responsibility for the helpless and lost would take over my life.

I knew that if I stopped to rescue a stray dog, I implicitly agreed to foster him or her. So many well-meaning people will go so far as to pick up a stray, but then drive directly to the Humane Society and expect to unload their responsibility on someone else. People unfamiliar with shelter capacity limits, waiting lists, and foster home scarcity seem genuinely shocked when they can't just drop off a stray. I knew better. It was with full awareness of my commitment when I stopped for the black and white dog who turned out to be such a lovable clown. If a pair of soulful eyes looking up at you from a droopy face doesn't melt your heart, check your pulse.

A flash of black and white caught the corner of my eye as I drove the speed limit, a brisk forty-five miles per hour. I slammed on the brakes, shifted to park, and turned to look out the passenger side window. A beautiful little basset hound trotted next to the shoulder of the road, five feet from passing traffic. Her coloring resembled a cow in miniature. I pulled over, hopped out of the van, and greeted the little dog as she approached.

"And where do you think you're going?" I asked her. She stopped and looked up at me, tail wagging furiously. "So, are you friendly? As I reached down to pet her, she gave her reply; she lay on the ground, rolled over onto her back, and exposed her belly, as if to say, rub me.

"Too bad you're shy around strangers, girl."

 She wore no collar, so I coaxed her to follow me to the nearest front door. Despite the several cars in the driveway, no one answered the doorbell or my knocking. I had no means to identify the dog's owner. She was covered in fleas; I managed to pick off a tick before it burrowed into her skin. I went door to door, but no neighbor claimed the dog. She was officially lost or abandoned.

This beautiful stray could have become road kill. I decided to take the dog with me. I knew immediately that meant we would make room for just one more in our home while we looked for her owners. She would be placed in the lost and found postings and kept safe through the Humane Society's ten-day waiting period that allowed time for families to come looking for their lost pets. I knew if the owners seriously tried to find their dog, they would check with animal control. We notify the county animal shelter whenever we intake a stray dog or cat, providing a description of the animal, in case the owner checks there first.

I drove to the Humane Society shelter and had her scanned for a microchip, which she didn't have. The staff at the shelter gave her a round of shots, not knowing her vaccination history. I took her home, gave her a bath, and named her Bessie the Basset Hound. My wife and I have fostered so many animals over the last several years that a new name for a stray becomes hard to find. Once we'd used a name on one animal passing through our refuge, calling a new critter with a recycled name didn't seem right. We may eventually have to violate that standard when we finally run out of names, but we didn't have a problem naming Bessie the Basset Hound. She looked like a Bessie.

If we had to describe Bessie in one word, adorable would work, but sweet comes in a close second. A very gentle, affectionate animal, she blended in with our six-pack of dogs as if she belonged. Bessie just didn't have a confrontational bone in her body. But no dog is perfect. Despite her gentle nature, Bessie had powerful jaws and strong teeth... and she knew how to use them.

One day an odd noise echoed through the house: Er-ER-Er-ER-Er-ER. The sound stopped for a while, but started again. Searching for its source, I found it came from Bessie, who trapped a Sponge-Bob Square Pants squeaky toy between her front paws. I recognized the sound of rubber being stretched past the breaking point, but still jumped at the loud POP! that followed.

Adorable Bessie rolled her apologetic eyes up at me and seemed very much as if she felt remorse. She pursed her lips. Pthew! She expelled the piece of rubber she'd bitten off well across the room. In that moment, I learned that dogs could spit.

Lisa suggested Bessie would be adopted quicker if visitors to the shelter could meet her. She was right. I wanted so much to keep her, but we have a large pack, important to be able to feed and keep them all healthy. We also performed periodic dental cleanings for our older dogs, requiring anesthesia. People don't understand why the anesthetic is necessary until they envision brushing a dog's teeth against its will. But the animal's long term health includes cleaning and maintenance of their teeth. And Bessie had teeth.

After she'd been with us a couple of weeks, on this Sunday, my wife and I went to church and wanted to go out to dinner afterwards. We checked the dog pack, and let everybody out to do  his or her business, and then we left. I made a fatal mistake, leaving Bessie unsupervised. I knew by this time that Bessie acted offended when we came and left home — again — so quickly. She expressed her displeasure on our TV remote control. Actually, Bessie obliterated it. We found its five thousand deconstructed pieces. Each of the buttons had been extracted; I got a mental picture of the dog as she spat out the numbers, one by one. How could I get angry?

I stood over the carnage and called, "Oh, Lisa." She laughed as soon as she saw the pile of rubble. Bessie wagged her tail with enthusiasm. I tried to scold her, but my face wouldn't stay straight. Lisa didn't exactly help. When sweet Bessie flopped rolled onto her back. I knew this was an invitation to scratch her belly. She showed no sign of guilt.

I relented soon after and agreed with Lisa to take Bessie to adoption events. Her exposure to the public shortened her tenure with us. To see her picture is to be smitten; to meet Bessie in person means falling in love. Her new human- beings have done exactly that. Re-christened Miss Daisy, our beautiful basset foster rules the roost in her new home. Occasionally we receive pictures of her, lounging in the sun or on the family couch, always ready to roll over and receive her belly rub.

CHAPTER 15
A REAL TROOOPER

Our involvement with our Humane Society continued to grow. My wife was elected to the board of directors and eventually became president of the organization. We lived, breathed, and slept animal rescue. Every email, voice mail, or knock at the door was a potential new desperate case. Phone calls came at all hours of the day and night.

Working in a leadership role for a small Humane Society able to afford only a few paid shelter employees meant the volunteer board of directors was responsible for everything from fundraising to computer support to hosting tours for Boy Scout troops. In a labor of love, many dedicated people in this small group gave up time, money, leisure and other interests to keep the shelter's doors open.

Lisa also worked a demanding full-time day job in the computer software industry. She often joked that she had two full-time jobs, one that paid her and one called the Humane Society. After struggling financially for a few years after the real estate market bust, my own writing career was getting off the ground.

It was in the midst of this all-consuming involvement that Trooper came into our lives. His story is appropriately told from Lisa's perspective.

Fostering often presented us with challenges in behavior rehabilitation, but sometimes we faced the more daunting task of healing broken bodies and making difficult choices.

If cats have nine lives, how many does a dog have?

Decisions of life and death take their toll on me. It's not easy to be president of our small county's Humane Society.

I recognized her phone number on the call display. "Lisa, thank God you answered your phone."

"Hi, Lauren. What's the matter?"

"I just found a dog that was hit by a car lying on the side of the road. I thought he might already be dead. I only stopped and got out to make sure there was nothing I could do. I really can't believe he's still alive. The poor thing ... his legs were all twisted and his body is scraped and bloody. Even the skin on his nose is rubbed off. The worst is his head injury. It breaks my heart to see how badly he's hurt—at first I was sure he was dead. But as I turned back toward my car, I saw his chest move."

Lauren finally paused to take a breath before plowing forward. "Lisa, he evacuated his bowels. I had some rags in my trunk and cleaned him up as best I could... but he's dying. Please, can the Humane Society help him? I don't know where else to take him or what to do."

Her torrent of words hit me like a hammer. Another good-hearted volunteer with yet another crisis. How could I say no? A dog was suffering.

We operate a small, no-kill rescue shelter. Most of our volunteers will stop to help a live dog running loose on the road, but who stops for a dead dog?

My guess is only the ones who have hearts of gold.

Lauren sounded calm, but her voice cracked with emotion. We both knew bowel evacuation usually portended death.

I asked Lauren a couple of questions to help me decide which vet would be closest.

"Yes, Lauren. We'll try to help the dog. Do you know Dr. McGruder at Crestview Animal Hospital? His clinic is closest to you, and they'll take really good care of him. I'll call ahead to let them know you're on your way."

I prayed the dog would live long enough to reach Crestview.

Our Humane Society is a non-profit organization with limited resources. Our sole purpose is to save lives, but which ones?

If his injuries are too severe for the dog to recover enough to enjoy life, the humane thing will be to euthanize him. Dr. McGruder is well aware of our limited budget and supports what we do. He'll give me good advice; know the right thing to do. I can't stand the idea of any animal suffering needlessly.

I took a deep breath and made the call.

Lauren arrived at the clinic with the dog while I was still on the phone. The receptionist offered to call me back after he had been evaluated.

Within an hour, the receptionist called me back as promised. After we spoke briefly, she put me on hold.

Dr. McGruder came on the line. He seems cantankerous to some people, but I know under his gruff exterior beats a heart of gold.

"His current condition is extremely critical, but stable. We've given him pain medication and we'll be monitoring his condition closely. I had to splint his front paw. It's too early to tell the extent of any brain damage. He can't be sedated to operate on the leg because of the risk of permanent damage from the injury to his brain. I'm worried about swelling. We'll keep him comfortable and monitor his progress. I'll call you tomorrow and give you an update."

The dog survived transport to the veterinary hospital. We assigned him a number and entered him into our database as an official Humane Society dog. He became D5747 for tracking purposes. Dogs don't respond to names like D5747. Because no one knew anything about the dog prior to Lauren finding him, I named him Trooper for his perseverance and will to live.

Trooper survived his first night at Crestview.

The following morning Dr. McGruder called as promised. "He's still alive, but he can't sit up, eat, or control his head."

My stomach knotted. Dr. McGruder doesn't mince words. He's painting a grim picture.

Anticipating the worst, I asked, "What's your recommendation?"

"It's still a little too early to tell. Basically, we're just boarding and monitoring the dog to make sure he doesn't suffer needless pain. I'm giving him intravenous pain meds in the fluids we're giving to keep him hydrated. He doesn't seem to be able to drink water yet. It's not expensive to board him. We can continue to treat his symptoms. Let's give it time and see."

Silently, I breathed a sigh of relief. I was pulling for him, but experience with reality told me not to let my hopes get too high.

And I wasn't the only one concerned about Trooper's welfare. Lauren asked for email updates on his condition, and his story spread among our family of volunteers associated with the shelter.

A decision on whether to surgically repair or amputate the leg had to wait until the dog stood a better chance of survival.

The next few days depended entirely on Trooper's determination to survive.

 People pestered me for updates on Trooper's condition, and the vet's receptionist was inundated with phone calls requesting information. I blasted an email to our interested well-wishers, promising regular updates if they would stop calling.

Trooper's new fan club rejoiced at the news the following day when his condition improved slightly. The day after, we all cheered when we learned he could drink water.

One especially sobering concern involved how his head lolled and pitched without warning. If he couldn't even control the movements of his head, how could this dog ever have quality of life?

As we fretted, slowly but surely, Trooper regained better control of his head. Not long after, he started eating solid food. Eventually, he sat up without help, but only stood with assistance. The staff at Crestview cheered every accomplishment, along with his growing fan club.

Then his steady, almost daily improvement came to a screeching halt. Trooper reached a plateau. And he still couldn't walk. Days passed. Dr. McGruder grew more and more concerned. The dog had progressed so well, until now. He wondered why the dog couldn't stand by itself.

To make matters worse, Trooper began to show signs of fear aggression during treatments and examinations. His new behavior raised major concern. He snapped and snarled at Dr. McGruder. I worried the efforts to save Trooper had been in vain, now that the dog demonstrated potential behavioral problems.

Without access to the dog's history, for all we knew, he could have been feral before the car ran over him. All our efforts might have been wasted.

It was also possible he could have been friendly prior to the brain injury, but the trauma changed his personality.

Yet a third possibility existed; the dog might simply still be sore. His therapy could be causing him pain.

Dr. McGruder warned his staff to be careful handling the dog. Gradually, Trooper calmed and his attitude toward people improved. He licked the palm of his handler when the opportunity arose, and the display of affection encouraged all of us.

Meanwhile, Lauren went door-to-door through the neighborhood near where the dog had been injured, searching in vain for his owner. She finally found a homeowner who claimed he saw the dog running loose and put out food for it to eat. However, he said the dog remained skittish and refused to be caught.

The neighbor speculated that Trooper's previous owners dumped him like useless junk near the entrance to the subdivision. There he waited in vain for their return, until the fateful accident.

Lauren blistered my ear telling me what she learned. She made a sincere effort to find Trooper's owners, and felt certain he had been purposefully abandoned.

Dr. McGruder started to suspect Trooper's inability to stand might be related to his life prior to the accident. He could have been an outside dog. That would explain his inability to stand on slick indoor tile flooring. He carried Trooper outside. The terse but wise vet was right. Trooper stood on grass without assistance, even with his leg in a splint.

Two long weeks passed while Trooper gradually improved. Although he still required additional care, the vet believed recovery in a home environment would be more comfortable. Plus, the dog needed socialization, and it would save our Humane Society precious funds that could be used to help other animals.

As a precautionary measure, I decided Trooper should temporarily come into my home for further evaluation of potential behavioral challenges.

Finally, Trooper left the hospital go home — my home. My husband has experience working with dog behavioral issues and he agreed to evaluate Trooper.

The rest of his recovery would be up to him.

When my husband, John, first met Trooper at Crestview, the frightened dog barked at him continuously. John calmly sat on the floor, refraining from eye contact with the dog. That allowed Trooper to become comfortable in his presence. After some time, Trooper inched close enough to gently sniff John's head. When Dr. McGruder joined them, the dog jumped to his side and clung to his leg like a small child.

Dr. McGruder frowned. "It may be best to have a veterinary technician the dog trusts help you get him into your car."

As he drove home, John wondered how he would get the dog with a questionable reputation out of his car without being bitten. He called me to discuss the problem. "I had helped getting the dog into the car, but I hadn't thought of making a plan for getting him out of car." John chuckled. "I guess I don't need to worry about the dog running away. With his splinted let slowing him down, I can outrun him if he tries to escape."

Any worries about receiving a serious bite from the little dog vanished on the way home. About halfway there, the dog inched close enough to rest his muzzle on John's elbow perched on the arm rest.

John called me back to report the latest development. "I seriously doubt Trooper is going to be a problem."

"Why do you say that?"

"He's a little love bug. He's snuggling with me."

Trooper acclimated and relaxed in his new environment. He demonstrated a strong desire for affection. John believed the dog had never been wild or feral, just neglected and underappreciated. The dog was so adorable and his story heart-rending, we both felt confident Trooper would attract a lot of interest when ready and well enough to attend adoption events.

During the long weekend spent with John and our dog pack, Trooper showed zero aggression for food, people, or other dogs. His scars only made him more interesting. He house-trained easily, never once having an "accident" indoors.

I passed the good news along the volunteer grapevine — Trooper received great reviews on his evaluation! A collective sigh of relief could be heard throughout the county.

After a long weekend of behavior evaluation, I look Trooper back to Crestview to have his injured leg re-evaluated. After his examination, we drove to meet someone very special. I let Trooper out of my van. His first steps gravitated toward the strange house, but tentatively. Lauren came outside to greet us. She took one look at Trooper and melted, saying, "Oh, Trooper!"

The emotion in her voice drew him. He hobbled to her side, tail wagging furiously, giving his best effort to leap for joy. Though he'd never gained consciousness the night she rescued him, he seemed to recognize her voice. Tears welled in Lauren's eyes at the sight of how well Trooper's recovery had progressed. I felt really good about having committed Humane Society resources to help save this dog.

With a bittersweet passing of the baton, I left the heroic little dog with Lauren. She asked to be his foster and earned the right as the one who picked his broken body off the street. As I drove away, I couldn't help but wonder if Trooper had already found his forever home. Only time would tell.

So, how many lives does a dog have? If he could answer, Trooper would surely say at least two. The best was saved for last.

CHAPTER 16
SHILOH'S ACCIDENT

Our dog Shiloh might not be the sharpest tool in the shed, but we love him dearly. He's the goofball of our pack, a giant galoot of a German Shepherd with a staggering number of genetic defects due to unscrupulous overbreeding. He looks ferocious and his bark is intimidating, but the image he projects is in stark contrast with his sweet and gentle personality.

Shiloh suffers from several physical maladies, but never acts like he's in pain. He's one tough cookie. We keep him as healthy as possible. We watch his weight and give him regular exercise in walks. True, not everybody would put up with his quirks and eccentric behavior. Shiloh's powerful bark rattles the windows of our house daily at the crack of dawn, alerting us of the onset of morning traffic... especially motorcycles and school buses. He barks at cars, trucks, joggers, clouds, and butterflies — anything on the move, because he always wants to go along for the ride.

My heart skipped a beat when I noticed the open fence gate. The exterminator had visited earlier in the day and apparently he hadn't closed the gate well enough when he left our backyard. I rushed back inside the house to do a quick head count. I checked every corner of every room with a rising dread in the pit of my stomach.

Three of our dogs were missing.

The timing of their escape couldn't have been worse. It was approaching the late afternoon rush hour, and we live near a busy road. I shouted for my son Matt, who happened to be home on a break between classes and work. We decided to split up and look for the dogs, each of us heading off in the opposite direction to search for our fugitives.

I jumped in the van and rolled down the windows. As I drove slowly down the street, I called out the names of our missing dogs, hoping to find them before the flood of commuters started coming home for the day. Matt took off on foot in the opposite direction, running around the block following the route we normally walked the pack.

Matt found Shiloh first. "Dad! Come quick! Shiloh's been hit by a car. He's hurt really bad," he said from his cell phone.

Those are the most horrible words an animal lover can hear about any dog, but devastating when the dog in question was Shiloh. My stomach churned, but I tried to stay calm. "Where are you?" I asked.

Of all our rescued pack members, Shiloh had the most special needs. He could least afford to be involved in a serious accident. The large but goofy German Shepherd with a gentle disposition comfortably blended in with the other misfits that make up our pack. The overbreeding that is unfortunately all too common in many popular dog breeds had ruined the genetic makeup of the poor dog. His lower spine was malformed and he suffered from dysplasia in both of his hips. Although he stood taller at the shoulder than any of our dogs, his back sloped dramatically down to his hips and his loose joints gave him a shaky, swaying gait.

Matt said that he and Shiloh were in a neighbor's car, not very far from our house, so I turned the van around. As I drove back toward home to find them, Matt began to describe Shiloh's injuries in graphic detail. "Shiloh was hit in the face. Blood's dripping from his mouth. And Dad — his back leg is mangled. I don't think he can walk."

His injuries sounded like they couldn't be worse. Hit in the head and his back legs run over? How is Shiloh still alive? Why was anyone going that fast in the neighborhood? Why didn't they stop to help my dog?

I braced myself for the worst. I was afraid that our lovable goofball might not recover. He might have to be euthanized. We'd always been exceptionally concerned about his frail physique — an accidental fall and broken hip would probably make it all but impossible for him ever to walk again. We had "Shiloh-proofed" our house by adding carpet runners on the wood floors, and added an extra door and a shorter flight of steps off the garage, into our backyard. The big dog might look formidable, but his body was as fragile as porcelain.

The thought of Shiloh suffering in pain made me ill, but so did the idea of ending his life prematurely. With any other of our dogs, my mind would have latched onto images of leg splints and recuperation, but Shiloh's legs might never mend properly. If he lost the use of even one of his hind legs, how would Shiloh be able to walk or even stand on his own? He could live in constant pain from his injuries. I pushed the disturbing thoughts aside. If and when the time came, I would make whatever decision was in Shiloh's best interest. In the meantime, the only thing that was important was getting him to the vet for examination and treatment as soon as possible.

I remembered how Shiloh had come into our lives. When I first saw him, he was living isolated in a large, fenced pen on top of a concrete slab. His owner had declared that he planned to "get rid of the dog" so he could keep another one that I had brought with me for him to adopt. Those words alone would make the prospective adoption home visit a short one. The man went on, complaining that Shiloh barked too much. I noticed an open

wound on the dog's foot and pointed it out, but his owner seemed disinterested in having the injury treated. Instead of leaving him with another dog, I convinced him to let me take Shiloh away from him.

We briefly fostered Shiloh for adoption through our local Humane Society, until the vet diagnosed the hip dysplasia. A trip to the specialists at the UGA veterinary school told us that he would need more than fifteen thousand dollars of surgery to repair all of his physical ailments, exceeding the abilities and budget of our little rescue group. My wife and I recognized that Shiloh would always have special needs, so we bought foam dog beds for his comfort, changed the flooring in our house to a friendlier surface for his hips, and accepted the fact that we had one more dog with nowhere else to go.

As I remembered how Shiloh ended up with us, I refused to think about the decisions that might be coming. My only concern was getting him to the vet, and finding our other two missing dogs. I dreaded even looking into Shiloh's eyes, after Matt's gruesome description. I knew that I would do everything possible to see him through the accident.

Matt lifted the big dog out of our neighbor's car, carried him over, and gently placed him in the back of our van. Shiloh never even whimpered. The only noise Shiloh made almost sounded like a squeal of delight, as if he was excited to be going for a car ride.

"Don't worry, I'll find the other dogs," said Matt. "Call me and let me know what the vet says."

As I drove toward the animal hospital, I called to give them advance notice that I was rushing in with a dog that had been hit by a car, and needed an emergency appointment to see the vet. After I hung up I thought to myself, Shiloh sure is one tough cookie. He's hasn't even whimpered, and he's got to be in serious pain.

I was astonished when Shiloh wobbled up to me from his spot in the back of the van and tried to jump into the front seat. "Shiloh, stop it! You're gonna hurt yourself even worse. You can't get in the front seat." I used my free arm to block the gap between the driver and passenger seats, but he slammed into it, nearly dislocating my elbow in the process. He might be hurt, but he didn't seem to know it. Impatiently, he pushed my arm, trying to bat it out of the way with his muzzle. "No! You can't get up here," I said, nearly missing the turn into the parking lot.

When I slid open the side door to the van, Shiloh jumped out as if nothing was wrong. I grabbed his collar and attached the leash, then stepped back to look at him. He didn't show any signs of having difficulties with his back legs. In fact, there didn't seem to be a mark on him.

Surprised and curious, I called Matt. "I found the other two dogs," he said without preamble. "Everybody's home, safe and sound. I didn't have any trouble finding them, by the way. Gracie and Sasha wandered back into the yard on their own. How's Shiloh?"

"Um…we haven't seen the vet yet. Which leg got mangled? He seems to be walking just fine."

"The one that's all bloody," Matt said with an exasperated sigh.

"Huh… he's not bleeding," I said. "In fact, I don't see any blood on him, at all. It looks like maybe he bit his tongue. But it quit bleeding, if he did."

"I don't know what to tell you," Matt said.

"I'll call you back after Dr. McGruder checks him out," I said. "We just got to his office. I'd better get him checked, just to be safe, in case he's got internal injuries or something," I said with a growing doubt.

Dr. McGruder checked Shiloh over thoroughly and confirmed my suspicions. "He's a very lucky dog. He'll be fine. Won't even need a stitch in that tongue," he said. Then he laughed. "He's a big boy. Maybe the car got hurt worse than he did."

I breathed a sigh of relief. There would be no difficult choices to make. Our lumbering clown of a dog could go back to barking at clouds and trying to catch shadows in his teeth.

Once Shiloh was safely back at the house, gnawing on a chew treat to comfort him after his traumatic experience, I went to the grocery store and bought a six-pack of beer. I took the six-pack over to my neighbor to thank him for his willingness to help both my dog and son. Not just anyone would put a strange dog into their own car and rush them to get help.

"How's your dog?" my neighbor asked, after I introduced myself.

"Shiloh will be fine," I said. "Apparently the car wasn't going very fast when it hit him."

"It wasn't a car, it was a truck."

"What?" I was shocked.

"Yep. Actually, it was a UPS truck," my neighbor said with an odd smile.

"What?" I repeated. "I can't believe a driver for UPS would hit my dog and just leave him lying there," I said incredulously. "I should call their offices right now and complain," I snapped, the unnecessary expense of the vet's bill still fresh in my mind.

"You could, but that's not what happened," my neighbor laughed. "The truck didn't hit him. He came to a complete stop, just fine. Your dog bolted into the street and ran right into that truck, face first, right into the grill. He even tried to bite the front bumper on the truck. The driver was afraid to get out of his truck. And you know they don't have doors on those things. Old Shiloh really scared the crap out of that UPS guy."

I felt bad for the driver, but this version of the story sounded exactly like something our affable lunkhead would do. After years of barking at delivery trucks driving past our house, Shiloh had decided to catch one for himself.

CHAPTER 17
WYATT THE WONDER DOG

After years of fostering over one hundred dogs and cats through our Humane Society, my wife and I questioned whether keeping up that pace was taking its toll. As Ox aged, younger foster dogs sometimes challenged his status in the pack. The wear and tear on our house, floors and furniture was noticeable. Our own joints and muscles were not as flexible as they once were, our reflexes not quite as sharp when it came to snagging a wayward puppy away from danger or breaking up a dog fight. Perhaps it was time to slow down, to foster fewer dogs. But how? How would we be able to say "no" after so many years of being the "yes" of last resort?

There was no easy way out, no formula for scaling back, because we knew quite well what our involvement meant to every animal that crossed through our doorway over the years. And yet, animal rescue is not a sprint or even a marathon. It has to be a relay race. We knew it was time to pass the baton to others with more energy and stamina.

With heavy hearts and lives immeasurably richer for our fostering experiences, we agreed it was time to slow down.

While we continue to foster dogs in dire need of a temporary roof over their heads, their stays are shorter and less frequent. We will never go back to being a one-dog household. That would be dull.

To cement our decision, we officially adopted the foster dogs still in our care, bringing the size of our permanent pack to six. That may seem like an insane number to most people, and sometimes we would wholeheartedly agree. However, we made commitments to each of these dogs and we will honor those commitments. This is the story of dog number six.

Wyatt might be the most "normal" dog we made a permanent pack member. He could have been easily adopted, had he not demonstrated a powerful bond with our son. Their "bromance" continues...

"Dawson Forest is boarding a dog for the Humane Society," Lisa said.

Those were her exact words. They translated to say, "There's a dog being boarded that I want to bring home and foster."

"You promised we wouldn't foster any more animals until we got a bigger house, and we'd live in the county for whom we foster dogs. Our house is too small. We have a great pack as it is. The last time you brought home a dog, it was not housebroken. I can handle using a belly band to stop him from peeing in the house, but that idiot beagle wouldn't stop pooping in the house."

"I remember," Lisa said. "You didn't have to remind me. The only reason I asked if you might be interested is because he's a German Shepherd. And he's a really big dog, too big to be cooped up, boarded in a kennel all day. They don't get any outdoor time, you know."

The ice in my veins slowly began to thaw. Sensing my defenses had weakened, Lisa went for the kill. She closed in for the coup de grace. "He's been cooped up in boarding for a couple of weeks now. I'm worried that he could get a little kennel crazy. You don't have to worry. He's not a puppy; he's housebroken and obedience trained. If there's any problem assimilating him into our pack, we can swap him out with a smaller dog from the shelter, immediately. As soon as I start taking him to adoption events, somebody will grab this guy. The staff at Dawson Forest absolutely fell in love with Wyatt — that's his name. See? Here's a picture of him."

She spoke too quickly for me to interrupt. When I laid eyes on the smiling white German Shepherd in the picture, any remaining will to resist vanished. Immediately, I not only wanted to foster the dog, I wanted to keep him. If his disposition were as pleasant as the photo promised, he'd make a perfect complement to Ox. I'd have black and white German Shepherds.

I said, "He doesn't look all that big. See, the vet tech next to him is squatting down. We've got enough room for him to stay at our house a week or so."

We drove up together. The vet tech brought Wyatt outside to meet us on a rope lead. I took it from her hand and proceeded to get dragged around the front yard like a rag doll. Lisa signed a couple of papers, and we were on our way home with one jubilant German Shepherd.

I let Wyatt loose in our backyard to let him acclimate, do any business he needed to get out of the way, and relax a little before introducing him to the rest of the pack. To my surprise, he exuberantly began running laps around the perimeter as fast as he could go, overjoyed with his new freedom to run and do as he pleased. Wyatt demonstrated his athleticism and speed, reveling in the moment.

The rest of the pack knew a new dog was running loose in their domain and desperately wanted to investigate. I decided on a pecking order for introductions, and thought it best that they took place in open space where it would be easier to separate the two dogs if a fight broke out. Armed with my trusty tennis racquet as the tool to create space without injury, I brought out Sasha, our newest addition. The gorgeous piebald Siberian Husky came from a friend forced to relocate to the other side of the country. Her new place would not allow the dog, and she had been desperate to find a good home for Sasha, who gets along well with every dog, cat, or human she meets. I had no worries about how Sasha would react to Wyatt, only vice-versa.

Wyatt interrupted his exercise regimen to greet Sasha nose-to-nose, tail wagging. From knowledge acquired by years of fostering now, I knew  better than to relax just yet. My concerns vanished when Wyatt communicated in dog-speak to Sasha that he would enjoy his exercise infinitely more if she would chase him, so that he had the sensation of running for his life. She obliged until her conditioning left her panting for air. She stood still while Wyatt still circled the yard, only lunging in his direction when his circuit brought him near enough that it took minimal effort.

Sasha has a remarkable persistence when speaking canine to me and her technique is unique. I know she's "talking" to me when she hunches low to the ground with her front end but leaves her tail in the air before she begins her "whoo-woo-woo...whoo" speak. She invariably ends up getting what she wants by barking until I say the right word, like "treat" or "walk," at which time she lets me know she is pleased that I figured out the right answer. I swear, this dog would give me the reward, if she only had opposable thumbs.

In this case, Sasha wanted reinforcements because Wyatt wore her out. I brought out Gracie, and sure enough, soon Wyatt was flying around the yard at top speed, with an overweight dog less than half his size in hot pursuit. Assimilation into the pack wasn't going to be a problem for this big baby. He only wanted to play.

I would say that I am more an expert on dog behavior than dog genetics. I might not be able to identify the specific gene sequence that differentiates a pit bull from a border collie, but I can easily identify one breed from the other on sight. More importantly, I'm more likely than your average scientist to be able to tell you which dog is more likely to bite you, and why — exactly what you've done to deserve it.

Caring for more than seventy different dogs in about a four-year period has given me a great deal of experience with a variety of breeds. On the other hand, as Clint Eastwood famously suggested, "A man's got to know his limitations."

I'm not an expert in veterinary medicine, a geneticist, or a breeder. I do not provide my pack medical care. Instead, I trust the expertise of the veterinarian I know well from working with the Humane Society.

He's a smart guy. He knows a lot about dogs, cats, and horses.

Therefore, I took Wyatt to my vet for a routine checkup, and to ask why he retained fecal matter caked under his tail, looking for both the cause and cure.

After thoroughly examining our new addition, my vet said the problem was genetic. He explained that Wyatt's cupped tail was due to poor breeding. He showed me how to clean the affected area and told me to get used to the idea. Terrific!

I'd just learned I'd just made a lifelong commitment to a dog with an unfortunate, permanent sanitary issue that would require my regular attention. Crudely put, I was going to have to wipe my dog's butt after he used the bathroom.

But soon I realized his true problem was that he'd been raised with an overly firm hand.

The first week we cleaned him as instructed. We've never had to clean him again.

Once Wyatt fully acclimated to pack behavior, he realized our rules were not quite as strict as what he experienced in his previous life. He relaxed. His tail now longer cupped because he no longer cowered in constant fear.

After his tail straightened, the problem vanished.

On our next visit, I told our vet about the non-existent problem, reminding him of his "genetic" diagnosis.

He laughed and said, "Hey, what do I know?"

After years of advanced education and decades of practice my vet knows more than most, but still not enough to explain all there is to know about dogs.

CHAPTER 18
BLOSSOM

So how do two perfectly sane people, recently retired from the front lines of dog fostering, manage to add a crazy cat to an already questionable six-pack of dogs?

I guess you had to be there.

As I first suggested in the introduction, Blossom is not your ordinary cat. As a result, she has become the only feline member of our pack. It helps that she finally decided that she loves me.

I'm not really a cat person. That's okay; Blossom isn't really a people sort of cat.

Her story began when a little old lady stopped by the Humane Society Thrift Store and asked to speak with the store manager. Joyce, the newly elected president of our board of directors, happened to be working in the store. A fellow member of the board, I was also volunteering in the new thrift store. My teenaged son Matthew was running the cash register at the front counter.

Joyce asked the elderly lady if she could be of assistance. She responded that she needed to surrender her cat.

Joyce explained, "We don't have room in our shelter at the moment. There is a waiting list for cats right now. We'll need some time to find a foster home. Can you keep the cat until we can find someone else to take her in foster care?"

The old lady protested, "The assisted living facility where I live will add an additional charge to my room fees every day for as long as the cat continues to live with me. I don't want to take her to animal control, but I can't afford to keep her."

Joyce was wavering and called me over to ask my opinion, or perhaps to strengthen her already waning resolve. "She says the cat is a Maine Coon. I know we agreed not to do animal intakes here at the Thrift Store, but do you want to take a look at it?"

I walked over, envisioning Cole, the Maine Coon who lived at our Humane Society adoption center. Cole served as the shelter mascot, a favorite of our staff and volunteers.

Cole hadn't been adopted long ago for only one reason. His special needs made for special expenses. Cole was diabetic and required a shot of insulin twice each day. Everyone loved Cole. Unlike the other shelter cats, he enjoyed the freedom to roam the office and hallways, his bed sequestered in our laundry room, in a place of honor befitting his stature.

His distinctive, fluffy raccoon-looking tail accessorized his grey-and-black tabby markings on Persian-length fur. Cole was heavy; I assumed because of the diabetes. He stood out in my mind; a great cat with a great personality. Cole was a laid-back fat cat.

Joyce said, "Maine Coon," so naturally I thought of Cole.

We walked over to the woman's car. "Can I see the cat?" I asked.

She slipped into the driver's seat and opened the wicker basket on the passenger seat. She reached inside and pulled out Blossom, cradling the young cat in her arms as she stroked her.

She easily put the cat back in the basket and closed the lid. It looked so simple when she did it.

"She's so young!" I said to Joyce. "She doesn't look much more than a year old."

"I haven't had Blossom very long," the old woman volunteered. "She's a good kitty."

Joyce and I stepped away to discuss our problem. We were considering both breaking our own rules of operation for the new thrift store and the Humane Society shelter by accepting the cat there.

In the parking lot as I looked at Joyce, a fateful decision that would forever impact my future formed words that crossed my lips. I said, "A young cat like this should be easy to adopt. Let's take her inside just to make sure, but I believe that's a Maine Coon and she's still a baby."

Inside the store, Matthew reinforced our tentative decision to take Blossom. He exclaimed, "She looks just like a skinny version of Cole!"

Matthew has a soft spot for Cole. He even learned how to administer Cole's insulin shots on those occasions he worked at the shelter. He lobbied for fostering Blossom in our home.

There's only one problem — we have a small pack of dogs living in our house. I worried that even a temporary move to our home could become a death sentence for Blossom. Our second-in-command in the pack has a strong prey drive we control through discipline and limiting the number of temptations for him.

As pack leaders, we have to protect the whole pack. Can a cat join a pack of canines?

I figured at worst case it would only be for a week or so until another spot came available in our network of foster homes.

Safely inside the store, I reached in and lifted Blossom out of her basket. As she did with the little old lady, Blossom reclined passively in my arms for a moment, maybe two.

What happened next is kind of sketchy. Perhaps I stroked her fur somewhere she did not want to be touched. Apparently, that forbidden zone covers about ninety percent of her body.

Maybe I did nothing. Maybe Blossom doesn't always need a reason.

After about two seconds of holding Blossom, she objected violently, without warning. She dug her claws deep into my forearm and bit me repeatedly as her way of saying, put me down!

I complied, dropping her like a hot potato. The skittish cat immediately vanished into the 10,000 square foot maze of sale items in the thrift store.

My heart sank as I realized what I'd done. I assumed we'd never be able to catch the volatile feline. Given the way my arm burned with pain, I wasn't eager to add insult to injury. I let the others look while I nursed my wounds. I checked just to make sure I didn't need a tourniquet.

Fortunately, the little old lady managed to catch Blossom and bravely secured the cat back into her basket. But at what cost?

My experienced eye gauged her blood loss to be less than a pint, but not by much. Blossom didn't play favorites. The old woman paid a stiff price, just like me.

Assuring us that she did not need a transfusion, she put the basket in our trusted hands.

Was her trust misplaced?

Joyce rushed off to the vet with Blossom to have her vaccinated and her nails clipped.

I now knew she was just a baby, but one with razor sharp claws.

Word spread like wildfire that we'd accepted a surrendered cat at the thrift store. Anne, the shelter director, called us on it. Joyce and I were busted.

"The cat needs to come through the shelter for intake evaluation before we can accept her into the adoption program," Anne reminded us patiently.

Joyce groused about following the rules before begrudgingly changing direction to drive the cat up to the shelter, where she left Blossom.

Soon, Anne called us at the thrift store once more.

"This cat is feral!" she claimed. "Nobody can touch her."

"That's ridiculous," I replied. "I've held her in my arms."

Granted, it had only been for a few seconds and my arms were still bleeding profusely, but I wasn't about to admit I had made a mistake. "Just get her back in her crate and I'll come get her and take her to my house. I've handled that cat. She isn't feral!" I said defiantly.

Somehow, Anne managed to re-crate Blossom in one of our old, worn animal carriers and transported her to Pet Vet to be sedated, vaccinated, and spayed. The next day my wife Lisa went to pick her up.

The staff at Pet Vet knows Lisa quite well. They greeted her with raised eyebrows and bemused smiles when she announced she was there to pick up Blossom. The old carrier came out with Blossom inside. Bright red tape now adorned the spot above the door with the warning

CAUTION printed on it in large capital letters. Blossom appeared to be developing quite the reputation.

Our howling pack of dogs probably freaked her out when Blossom arrived at my house, though her mental condition was not exactly stable before she got there. She retreated under the guest bed, issuing a guttural growl as a warning if anyone approached.

She stayed there for almost a month, coming out to eat and use the litter box, but only if no one was in the room with her. I began to wonder if Anne had been right.

With her nails clipped, Blossom couldn't do quite as much damage. However, she still had teeth, which still made her scary. She made it clear she had no interest in becoming socialized.

Yet our son Matthew was determined to break the ice. I might have kept the status quo indefinitely. Patiently, he sat in her room while he used his laptop for hours on end and refused to give up on Blossom.

He discovered if he made any movement to pet her, she would hiss and spit. But if he ignored her, she seemed to get her feelings hurt.

His reverse psychology seemed to be working. The cat wanted to interact, but only on her terms. Within days, Matthew would feel her rub against his body. Yet if his hand moved to touch her, she'd slap at it before speeding away.

Her consistent antisocial behavior earned her first nickname — spawn of Satan.

She lived in our house for almost a month before we decided it was safe to let her out of the guest bedroom. "What do you think is wrong with her?" I asked Lisa.

"She probably was taken from her mother too young. Blossom doesn't really know how to be a cat. Oh, dear. We're never going to find a home for her!" my wife lamented.

For a cat that seemed remarkably antisocial when she first came to us, Blossom developed a dangerous habit. She constantly hovered in a favorite spot at the foot of the stairs. There she lounged just on the other side of a locking child gate I installed to block the stairwell and protect her from the dogs.

It seemed she enjoyed taunting them.

Actually, she taunted one — Ox. The rest of our pack knew to fear Blossom, giving her wide berth.

Not Ox. Enmity festered between Blossom and Ox.

One night Blossom jumped the bottom gate, apparently in dire need of an adrenaline rush. Ox chased her around the living room until the out-of-place flash of grey and black registered in Lisa's mind and she realized what was happening, alerting her to the inevitable disaster.

Lisa shouted, "Ox, NO!"

My flustered dog ran to my side as I worked in my home office, oblivious to the excitement.

Lisa scooped Blossom up into her arms and asked, "How's Mama's baby kitty?"

I wanted to warn her, she'll rip your face off, woman! Instead, I kept my tongue and watched in amazement as Lisa cooed and stroked the cat.

My second "pet" name for Blossom (the most inappropriately named cat in the world) was Norma Bates. This feline was definitely Psycho.

Lisa didn't like spawn of Satan, Psycho, or Norma Bates. She kept deluding herself with the idea the cat was friendly, always asking, "Where's Mama's baby kitty?"

I wondered exactly when and where my wife had lost her ever-loving mind. Baby kitty sounded innocent. And sweet.

The spawn of Satan? I didn't think she was sweet, not a bit.

But with jealousy, I couldn't help but notice Blossom preferred Lisa to me. I scooped her litter, changed the water in her dish, cut up and served her cooked chicken for dinner. Still, she might decide to bite the proverbial hand that fed her.

She played favorites with my wife, curling to sleep in the crook of Mama's leg. She was indeed, Mama's baby kitty. With razor sharp claws that had grown back.

After several months passed, we accepted that Blossom was a permanent addition to our home. I filled out the adoption paperwork.

I visited the local discount superstore and came home with a giant cat-climbing tree that Lisa mocked on sight. "Maine Coons don't like to climb. They aren't vertical because they are so large. You wasted our money," she informed me, having thoroughly done her research on Maine Coons.

Nobody told Blossom. Reminiscent of a lumberjack, she went straight up the center post of the towering contraption, using her claws like tree spikes. She scornfully ignored the small platforms designed to provide a set of stairs. There she perched atop her new prize, lording over my bedroom, issuing a guttural challenge to anyone to come within range and risk the wrath of the claw.

"This is MY bedroom, you fur ball!" I grumbled. "I bought you the damned thing!"

She growled back an ominous warning in response. Her ample girth now overflowed the confines of her roost. Recently I christened her yet again with a new nickname: "Philomena Fatcat" to mock her bloated and growing stomach. Her eyes flashed with thinly disguised hostility.

It was too early for the lunchtime snack.

I teased and provoked her, touching her exposed underbelly with my finger.

Proving deceptively quicker than her awkward looking pose suggested possible, she raked my hand. This time she failed to draw blood, though. She's getting slow.

Handling Blossom is not easy... I follow the same techniques most people use handling nitroglycerin. Extreme care is essential. Thick padded gloves are a tool of the trade.

Sometimes we must face an unpleasant reality. Occasionally we have to take Blossom to the vet. I discovered a cluster of horrible mats in Blossom's fur near the base of her tail. They could not be combed out, mostly because Blossom fled in terror at the sight of a brush or comb. It hurt Blossom to brush them; I figured out that if she was accidentally touched on those sensitive mats while being petted, it invariably provoked her to defend herself.

Lisa decided we needed to take Blossom to the vet for sedation prior to grooming. Otherwise, nobody would ever be able to touch her. From the grooming menu, Lisa ordered the lion cut.

That meant Blossom was shaved, from the back of her neck all over her body, with absurd tufts of fur left on her ankles and at the tip of her tail.

Her new look inspired yet another nickname, "Pom-Pom."

The funny thing is the new nickname didn't seem to make her so mad. Was it the mats that she objected to more than the petting? Now she even let me pet her.

One day she made a strange sound while I stroked her back. I withdrew my hand in alarm. "What's wrong with her?" I asked.

"She's purring," Lisa answered.

I'd never heard Blossom do that.

She has become much more affectionate now the hair mats no longer cause her discomfort. Touching her fur no longer causes pain when she's petted. The forbidden zone on Blossom has shrunk to less than ten percent of her body.

She's still a very strange cat, but that just means in our house, she fits right in. Blossom is the only cat I've ever known that thumps her paw on the floor like a dog when you scratch just the right spot behind her ear.

I think she even likes her new nickname. Her tail twitches in approval whenever she hears me say it. I don't let Lisa hear me, in case it upsets her.

I now call Blossom, "Daddy's baby kitty."

CHAPTER 19
TAKE THE BATON

Currently, Lisa and I no longer serve on the board of directors in our local Humane Society. We have taken a break to recharge the batteries, and allow time to heal some of the emotional wounds inevitable in this kind of front-line involvement in animal rescue. A new wave of capable volunteers now fills our shoes and the important work continues.

Last year, the county approved building a large new state-of-the-art animal shelter. A task force is working closely with animal rescue groups to move the county toward "no-kill community" status in the coming years. The fact that county officials even recognize the merit of doing so speaks volumes.

I believe the tide is turning.

A lot has changed in animal welfare since the stories in this book began in the late 1960's. The change is particularly dramatic in the South. My wife grew up in rural South Georgia, where dogs were always outside dogs and cats were only valued as utilitarian barn mousers. It was a journey of light years to her life today. Yet, her story repeats countless times in our generation and beyond. Our children and theirs will find the plight of 1960's companion animals unconscionable. They will value life and recognize the responsibility we have to the domesticated animals whose ancestors chose to align themselves with humans.

In Georgia, we often hear that the northeastern states are far ahead of us, rescue groups in those areas now often pulling animals from southern shelters because their own kennel space sits empty. From here, that is welcome news that portends a glorious future, because it means we are likely a decade or two away from having that enviable problem ourselves — empty kennels in our shelters here in the South.

But even if the entire United States reaches the goal of no homeless animals, the need for animal welfare advocates will continue. Our battle will move to other areas: individual cruelty cases, caring for the broken ones unadoptable for medical or behavior reasons, educating new generations on the importance of spay/neuter and medical preventatives, and drawing the line that says, "We will *not* go back."

My wife and I have temporarily scaled back our volunteer efforts while we work to relocate our house and pack closer to our extended family, to the Georgia coast where we plan to retire along with our dogs and cat. But we can never truly step away from a cause that has been such a huge part of our lives, only pause and transition in *how* we help.

Much work lies ahead for animal advocates.

It is time to pass the baton.

So, what can you do to help?

Get involved. Even if you only have one hour a week, visit your local shelter and become a volunteer. Take a dog that has been cooped up in a run all day for a walk on a leash (bring your own, just in case). Animal shelters need volunteers the most on traditional holidays like Christmas and Thanksgiving, when paid employees want time off to be with their families.

Foster a pet. The animal you bring into your home, even on a temporary basis, will provide the shelter an opportunity to save an additional life by creating an empty space. The vacant kennel is thus freed for use by another animal. If you assist the rescue group in efforts to market your foster pet and help find them a deserving home, you might be surprised how quickly the perfect forever home comes along. As you do, you will experience your own stories of unique, special animals as each one enriches your life in some way.

Financially support your local rescue groups. In times of economic downturn, charities are especially challenged to meet their budget demands, which increase with the influx of a higher volume of animals coming through than normal. With animal rescue groups, a significant problem is the increase in the number of owner-surrendered animals as people lose their jobs and homes, having no choice but to relocate. If your local Humane Society has a thrift store, donate items to them that have outgrown their usefulness to you.

If you cannot afford to give money, consider donating your time. Help your local rescue raise funds by planning events and raising community awareness among your friends and neighbors. Every dollar that you donate, help raise, or inspire someone else to give will help save a life.

If you nothing else and you enjoyed these stories, you can help your local animal rescue group by recommending that they contact Each Voice Publishing for information about acquiring the book at wholesale prices, forty percent off the retail price. They can resell this book to their supporters at the list price, as long as they use the net proceeds to help animals in your locale. This is about more than saving money; it's about saving lives.

Keep the big picture in proper perspective. If you have already committed to foster one animal, shut down the communication channels and stop listening to additional cries for help, until you have finished your commitment to help the one under your roof.

Pace your participation in order to avoid burn out and compassion fatigue. Accept the fact that you cannot help every homeless animal or save every life that pleads to you from your email inbox. But can you do more than you're currently doing?

There are many lives out there worth saving.

And remember, there is always a next one.

ABOUT THE AUTHOR

John L. Leonard was born in Savannah, Georgia and graduated from Savannah Christian School. He holds a BBA in Management Information Systems from the University of Georgia and worked as a computer programmer for more than twenty years before becoming a writer.

John has spent most of his adult life in the northern suburbs of Atlanta. His writing has also been influenced by shorter stints working as a bartender, real estate investor, and landlord. He has been married to wife Lisa for twenty-one years and is the proud father of two and grandfather of three, as well as pack leader for several wonderful dogs and a hostile Maine Coon cat. He and Lisa have also volunteered with their local Humane Society for a number of years, providing the inspiration for these short stories about their foster experiences.

His first non-fiction book debuted in 2010, *Divine Evolution*. His short story "The Hummingbird" is included in the *God Makes Lemonade* collection from Don Jacobson.

John also writes detective novels under the pen name Rocky Leonard. His first detective thriller in the Robert Mercer series, *Coastal Empire*, is available in ebook and paperback.

John was the only three-time gold medal award winner in the 2013 Readers' Favorite International Awards competition. His book, *Counterargument for God,* won in the Nonfiction/Religion and Philosophy category. His paranormal thriller, *Secondhand Sight,* won for Fiction/Horror, and this collection of short stories, *Always a Next One,* took the gold medal for Nonfiction/Animals.

The local color in his writing is equally authentic whether the setting is a Georgia beach, downtown Atlanta, or the Appalachian foothills in north Georgia.

Connect with John at www.southernprose.com

ORIGINALLY PUBLISHED

The following stories in this edition were originally published in whole or in part, in the anthology, *Hot Dogs and Cool Cats*, the author's contributions to the Writer's Alliance of Georgia (WAG)

MAGGIE DID IT TO HERSELF
HAIR TRIGGER
AMAZING GRACIE
SIMON/SIMONE
THE DOG WHO LIVED UNDER GRANDMA'S BED
SPITFIRE
A REAL TROOPER
THE CATFIGHT
MEMPHIS AND THE MIGHTY OX
BESSIE THE BASSET HOUND

DON'T MISS

The inaugural Robert Mercer Mystery
by Rocky Leonard

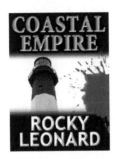

Available now at www.eachvoicepub.com

"You underestimate my desire, Mercer. I can always make you suffer in agony for a while before you die. Once you are out of the way, we can torch your house in case you hid them there. We'll spread around a little money. Lance probably knows a cop he can buy if we need to. Enough money and advance warning gives us time to do damage control," Yarborough shouted.

A second voice said, "Hey! I think I see something moving out there!"

Well, I guess that settles it, Mercer thought. Let the games begin.

"Let's see you control this damage," Mercer said as he stepped into the open.

# # #

Wealthy and beautiful Sarah Reid hires private detective Robert Mercer to investigate her husband Barry, a real estate mogul whom she believes may be unfaithful. Mercer embarks on a case of possible identity theft and probable murder. He uncovers a vicious web of real estate fraud and jewelry theft that leads him to Kelly, an alluring woman with a few secrets of her own.

As Mercer pieces the puzzle together, the dead bodies begin to pile up and events threaten to spin out of control. With his canine partner Ox, a large black German Shepherd Dog, and John Sutlive, an old Marine buddy, Mercer and his motley crew do battle with a small army of villains in a fight to the death for his client.

This novel, set in sultry and mysterious Savannah, Georgia, is the inaugural book in the Robert Mercer detective series of great mysteries with irresistible supernatural twists.

AMAZON.COM READERS RAVE ABOUT COASTAL EMPIRE

"Once I started reading, I couldn't put the book down. I loved the way that there were several stories that eventually all came together into one. Very creative and captivating mystery with great details and obvious knowledge about all of the material he was writing about including the locations, history, law, etc. There was never a dull moment and the book flowed very well. As soon as I finished, I started to read the next book by Rocky Leonard "Secondhand Sight" and can't wait to read more."

–Tori

"*Coastal Empire* is a fantastic novel, I couldn't put it down. Leonard masterfully sets the story up with tone and setting that settles in on the reader, making you feel like you're actually part of the story, then paints rich characters that are easy to care about. And the mystery is set up

perfectly, drawing the reader in even further. I truly enjoyed it and will definitely buy the next book Leonard puts out."
  —*Chris Lindberg, author of Code of Darkness*

Praise for Rocky Leonard's
SECONDHAND SIGHT

"What a riveting read! This book grabbed me from the first page...Leonard creates a thrilling and chilling murder mystery, with an intriguing touch of the paranormal...The threads pull together...to a harrowing climax...and in the midst of all the mayhem, people find themselves and each other...Murder mystery and paranormal fans will love this book."
—Readers' Favorite

"*Secondhand Sight* has all the elements of a good crime novel: a strong lead character, a sinister villain, bloody murder scenes plus the injection of the supernatural to add drama and mysticism to its dynamic plot."
—IP Book Reviewers

"An unexpected mix of police procedural, thriller, supernatural and horror."
—Kirkus Reviews

SECONDHAND SIGHT
by Rocky Leonard

Secondhand Sight won the 2013 Readers' Favorite International Book Awards gold medal for Fiction/Horror.

Dan Harper is just an ordinary guy, having an ordinary day...until he ruins his tie during lunch. When he visits a thrift store near his office for an inexpensive replacement, merely touching a secondhand tie triggers a flood of gruesome images only he can see. Are they hallucinations, or suppressed memories?

Dan desperately wants these visions to be nothing more than a product of his imagination, but soon enough, he discovers real crime scenes and murder victims. Dan can no longer ignore the unseen powers forcing him to confront the demons of his past. Dark forces prod him to seek the identity of the faceless murderer haunting his dreams.

Dan's worst fear is the suspicion he'll eventually confront the face of this brutal killer in last place he wants to look - the mirror.

This suspense thriller is a mix of police procedural with a paranormal twist.

23295341R00096

Made in the USA
San Bernardino, CA
12 August 2015